The Teen I Want to Be

Weekly Reader Books offers several exciting
card and activity programs. For information,
write to WEEKLY READER BOOKS, P.O. Box 16636,
Columbus, Ohio 43216.

MARY · ANN · GREEN

The Teen I Want to Be™

OLIVER
NELSON

A Division of Thomas Nelson Publishers
Nashville • Atlanta • Camden • New York

Published in Nashville, Tennessee, by Oliver-Nelson Books, a division of Thomas Nelson, Inc., Publishers, and distributed in Canada by Lawson Falle, Ltd., Cambridge, Ontario.

Printed in the United States of America.

The material in Chapter 8 is reproduced from the booklet *Accent On You* by permission of Tambrands Inc. Copyright © 1983 Tambrands Inc. All rights reserved.

Book design by Nancy Bozeman.

Illustrations by Robyn Carter, art instructor, Bauder Fashion College of Atlanta.
Photographs of Nancy Schaefer and Libby Trest by Larry Scaggs.
Photographs of Jodi Green by Brian Bieder. Teen Board picture courtesy of Rich's.
Models Lisa Overstreet, Abby Moore, Nancy Schaefer, and Dawn Parrish.
Exercises by Libby Trest.

Library of Congress Cataloging in Publication Data

Green, Mary Ann, 1936-
    The teen I want to be.

    Summary: An image consultant shares her ideas
for teen-age girls to become "the best me" in
clothes, hair, skin, and size; with time, money,
and other people.
    1. Beauty, Personal.   2. Adolescent girls—
health and hygiene.   3. Adolescent girls—Life
skills guide. [1. Beauty, Personal.   2. Adolescent
girls] I. Title.
RA778.G797 1985   646.7′042   85-21722
ISBN 0-8407-9040-6
ISBN 0-8407-9544-0 (pbk.)

2 3 4 5 6 7 8 9 10 - 97 96 95 94 93 92 91 90 89 88

♥

To my mother, ELIZABETH SPEIR,
who gave me the freedom to dream my dreams.

To my daughter, JODI ELIZABETH GREEN,
who is "a dream come true" for me. Jodi, you were a part of my childhood dreams many long years before you were born. I used to play house and dream about having a little girl someday. You have surpassed all of those dreams I had about a daughter. You have always been and are a joy to me. Thank you for being a part of my life.

CONTENTS

PART TWO: The Best Outer Me

INTRODUCTION

♥ No one ever said that it is easy to be a teen-ager because it isn't. Each part of the life's journey has its problems, and certainly youth has an abundance of them. You are sort of stuck in between. You are neither a child nor an adult, physically, mentally, or emotionally. You want desperately to be your own unique person, yet you need to be exactly like your friends. Everything seems so topsy-turvy. You have many wonderful dreams, but reality too often crushes them. I care about you and I'd like to help you through this confusing time in your life.

Who am I? I am Mary Ann Green, a mother, a fashion model, an image consultant, an author, and a teacher. I have been a director of modeling and finishing for two schools. My workshop "The Teen I Want to Be" has allowed me to speak to thousands of young girls like you all across America. I have found that dreams really do come true if you know how to make them come true. They have for me, and I want them to come true for you too!

As a teen-ager, you need to know someone in whom you can have confidence, someone you can go to for guidance. Having someone you can trust to share your innermost self with as you go through the exhilarating ups and the painful downs helps you to have a better perspective about yourself and your world. Girl talk is important!

That's why I want to talk to you about a lot of the things that I know are important to you. I wish that I could talk *with* you rather than *to* you, but since that is impossible, this book allows me to share my thoughts and some pointers with you. At times I'll probably sound like your teacher, sometimes I'll sound like a fashion authority, and lots of times I'll probably sound just like your mom. But most of all I want to be your friend—a friend who has gone through the same things you are going through. A friend who has also had the privilege of being involved again in the teen-age years with her own daughter, Jodi, whom you will meet in this book, as well as all the girls who have attended "The Teen I Want to Be" Workshops. As you read each page, you can be assured (and reassured) that you have a friend who believes in you and who cheers you on as you reach for and accomplish your *possible* dreams.

After you have finished reading this book, ask your mom to read it. I believe she will be supportive of you. She will also have fun with you as you begin to put into practice all the exciting things you are about to learn.

Thank you for permitting me to come into your life. I hope you will be motivated and inspired to new and possible dreams for yourself as you try out some of the things we will talk about. See how exciting life can be! Dream your dreams. Reach for the stars. There will never be another person on the face of the earth just like you. Apply the principles that you are about to learn and become the best *you* that you can be!

ACKNOWLEDGMENTS

♥ To all of you who are or ever have been in my life—you are a vital part of the process in my becoming the author of this book. And especially to Cecil Murphy.

To Donna Gordon, Jack and Margaret Boyd, and Lynn Pounds for help in the preparation of this manuscript.

To all of my friends, who so patiently stood by me and still loved me after being told over and over again, "Sorry, I have to work on the book today."

And especially to my husband Joe, who helped in more ways than I could mention. Without him I'm afraid this "dream" might not have come true!

CHAPTER ONE

how to
dream possible dreams

♥ Your silent world of thoughts and dreams belongs to you and to you alone. You hold the key. No one else can enter the door into your personal world unless you decide to open it. Though your dreams and thoughts are yours alone, even you may not know clearly what they are. They may all be a fuzzy, jumbled-up mess. If they are, don't leave them that way. I have some ideas to help you get to know yourself better. So what are we waiting for? Let's get started!

Get a pen or pencil, find a comfortable spot where you won't have any distractions, and settle down with me to do some dreaming. Let's pretend that we could magically make all your dreams come true. Wouldn't that be fun? Well, maybe we don't have time to tackle all your dreams right now. Let's take only the most important ones, the thoughts and dreams you have about yourself, your whole self.

Your whole self has to do with your inner self and your outer self. Your *inner self* is your mind (the way you think), your will (your decision to act), and your emotions (the way you feel). Another way of describing your inner self is to say it is your abilities, actions, and personality. Your *outer self* is your physical self.

DREAMS

First, dream about how you would like to be on the inside. This is for you and for no one else, so don't hold back. Write down everything.

• If my dreams could come true, I would like for the inner me (my abilities, actions, and personality) to be:

_____

_____

_____

_____

_____

Was that difficult? Now, dream about your outer self. If you could look exactly the way you wanted to, how would you look? (I bet this question will be easier to answer than the first one!) Which have you thought and dreamed about the most, your inner self or your outer self? If you are like most of the teen-agers in the workshops I conduct, you have dreamed a lot more about the way you would like to look.

• If my dreams could come true, I would like to look:

_____

_____

_____

_____

SELF-INVENTORY

Now that you have dreamed your dreams, I want you to do something else. To get to know yourself better, take a self-inventory in each area. What is the inner you actually like? What do you look like? Some people find it very painful to think about themselves this way. Are you like that? Try it, and you will find that you are not so bad after all. You already have many strengths and a lot of potential to make many of your dreams come true!

• The inner me (my abilities, actions, and personality) is the following way:

_____

_____

_____

_____

• I look the following ways:

_____

_____

_____

_____

Did you describe the way you look in such a way that if you were at a busy airport to meet someone you did not know, that person could recognize you by your description? Please don't take the easy way out and describe your clothes for identification—"I'll be the girl wearing a purple dress with chartreuse polka dots, and I'll have a red flower in my hair." Be sure you describe only the physical you.

Writing things down usually clears up a lot of that fuzzy mess we talked about earlier. After doing these exercises, you should know what your dreams are, and you should know yourself better. Can you say your dreams are a possibility for you? To determine this, do the following exercise.

POSSIBLE DREAMS AND IMPOSSIBLE DREAMS

1. Compare each quality of your inner self dreams with each quality of your inner self-inventory.
2. Determine point by point if they are the same or if they are different. Most of your dreams will probably be different.

16

3. When the dream is different from the inventory, ask yourself: Is there anything I can do or learn that will make my dream come true? Is my dream a possible dream?
4. If the answer is no, then it is an impossible dream. Take your pen and mark through the dream. If the answer is yes, put a check mark by the possible dream.
5. Repeat Steps 1 through 4 with the outer self.

Let me give you some examples so you will better understand what I want you to do.

INNER SELF

MY DREAMS   MY SELF-INVENTORY

Possible dream

I would like to be friendlier
and more outgoing   I am shy

OUTER SELF

MY DREAMS   MY SELF-INVENTORY

Impossible dream

I would like to be short   I am 5'9" tall

Are these examples possible or impossible dreams? You were right if you said, "The inner self dream is possible, and the outer self dream is impossible." (You can become a friendlier person, but you cannot change your height.) According to the instructions, put a check mark by the possible dream and mark through the impossible dream.

17

Take time now to compare your dreams and your self-inventory. The rest of the book will mean much more to you if you do because you will know the areas in your life you will need to accept and the ones you will want to work on.

Are you still not sure about possible and impossible dreams? See if you can tell which of the following are possible dreams and which are impossible dreams.

	Possible	Impossible
Change height.	☐	☐
Change eye color.	☐	☐
Change hair.	☐	☐
Change bone structure.	☐	☐
Change weight.	☐	☐
Be less shy.	☐	☐
Be in better physical shape.	☐	☐
Use mind better.	☐	☐
Change skin color.	☐	☐
Change teeth.	☐	☐
Change facial expression.	☐	☐
Change hands and feet.	☐	☐
Change fingernails and toenails.	☐	☐
Change grooming.	☐	☐
Change style of dress.	☐	☐

Change parents.	☐	☐
Change brothers and sisters.	☐	☐
Change friends.	☐	☐

Some things you can change, and some things you cannot change. It is very important for you to know the difference. Let's talk about a few of these statements.

Can you change your height? No (impossible dream).

Can you change your eye color? No (impossible dream). You might be thinking, *Yes, I could. I could wear colored contact lenses.* Can you make dark brown eyes look pale sky blue with contact lenses? No. There are definite limitations, and besides that, how many people would wear contact lenses to change eye color if they did not need to wear eyeglasses?

Can you change your hair? Yes and no (possible dream and impossible dream). You can change your hair style. You can color your hair, perm your hair, or relax your hair. You cannot change its basic texture, its thinness or thickness, and you cannot make it naturally straight or naturally curly.

Can you change your bone structure? No (impossible dream). You could have cosmetic surgery and change a few of your features, but you can't change every bone in your body.

Can you change your weight? Yes (possible dream). You can gain weight, or you can lose weight.

Can you be less shy? Yes (possible dream). You can learn how to be friendlier, determine to take action, and apply what you learn.

Can you be in better shape physically? Yes (possible dream). You can learn about nutrition and exercise and take action.

Can you use your mind better? Yes (possible dream). You can develop a desire for knowledge and learn better study habits.

Can you have a different color skin? No (impossible dream). You can suntan the skin you have, but you cannot change its basic color.

Are you beginning to get the picture now about what is changeable and what is unchangeable?

THOUGHTS

What do you spend the most time thinking about—your possible dreams or your impossible dreams? If you are typical of most of the girls in my workshops, you spend your time thinking about things that can never be changed. Have you ever had thoughts like these? *Oh, if I were only shorter and smaller boned like Cathy. Or I wish I didn't have all these freckles. I hate them! Or I wish my nose wasn't so wide. And this hair! Why did I have to be born with such curly hair? I wish I had straight, silky hair so I could wear the new style. And the color of my skin—yuk!*

COMPARISON

Do you ever compare yourself with other people? All the time, right? You think, *She's so pretty and I'm so ugly. She has such neat clothes, and mine are the pits. All the guys like her, and I can't even get one guy to like me. She has such a fun personality.* The comparison goes on and on until you end up having a big pity party—you get to the point where you go around feeling very sorry for yourself. And the more you think about yourself, the lower you get.

Believe me, you cannot win in the comparison game. It will get you down every time. You can never be like someone else, no matter how hard you try. Remember, you are unique. There is no one else like you in the world! Accept yourself, and work on being the best you.

"Accept myself? How?" You may ask. Begin by accepting those unchangeable "givens" in your life. Say to yourself, "This is the way I have been created. Therefore, I choose to believe there is a good reason for it. I accept all about me that I cannot change. I accept my givens." Now, take all the time and energy you use in dreaming impossible dreams and comparing yourself to others and direct them toward making your possible dreams come true. Just imagine what you would be like if you developed *all* your potential. WOW! Remember, never compare yourself to someone else.

COMPETITION

Competition is another activity that works against you, except in sports and games. If you feel you always have to be smarter, prettier, funnier, or whatever than everyone else, you are setting yourself up for a driven, lonely life. Being the best does not make you feel good about yourself or make you happy. You might think that if you could be the prettiest girl in your school, you would be the happiest person in the world. But that isn't so. Even most beauty queens have not accepted themselves. They have won the title for being the best, but inside they are afraid that other girls are really prettier than they are. They have their own long lists of unchangeable things that they would like to change too.

Be satisfied with yourself. Try not to compete with others—compete only with yourself. See how many of your possible dreams you can accomplish! Remember, you are of great worth as a person. When you try to measure up to someone else, you might forget that truth!

21

ACCEPTANCE

If your thoughts were exposed, would you be locked up because of cruelty to yourself? Do you criticize yourself and put yourself down all of the time? You wouldn't do that to others, so don't do that to yourself. Determine once and for all to accept and love yourself. Be your own best friend. Then you will be able to be a good friend to others. Change what you can change and accept what you cannot change. Make your possible dreams come true.

Be excited about all of who you are, both the changeable —and the unchangeable!

Keep telling yourself—
"The Teen I Want to Be"
is
the Best Me—
the very Best Me!

Notes

♥ work at not comparing myself to others

♥ accept my "givens"

♥ compete with myself only

♥ quit putting myself down

♥ change what I can & accept what I can't change

♥ become the BEST ME !!!

CHAPTER TWO

how to
make my dreams come true

♥ Your possible dreams really can come true in your life if you want them to. You can make them happen by learning how to put them into reachable goals, by thinking positively, and by managing your time wisely.

Look back over your list of dreams. The ones that you have marked through are your impossible dreams. You need to learn how to accept these things in your life that you *cannot* change. The dreams with a check mark beside them are your possible dreams. They are the things that you *can* change. List them all in the following space.

MY POSSIBLE DREAMS

• My Inner Self:

_____

_____

_____

• My Outer Self:

_____

_____

_____

Do you have other dreams you would like to make happen for yourself? Add them to the list—just be sure they are possible. Your list might look something like this one.

I want to

1. Be more outgoing.
2. Get along better with my family.
3. Stop putting myself down.
4. Solve some of my conflicts.
5. Be more positive.
6. Start exercising.
7. Work on my clothes for school.
8. Get a new hair style.
9. Learn how to take good care of my skin.
10. Learn how to apply my make-up.
11. Have better posture and a more graceful walk.
12. Be the Best Me—the very Best Me!

You must be willing to take action, or all of those desires on your list will remain unfulfilled dreams instead of dreams that come true.

24

The first thing you need to do is to renumber the items on your list in the order in which you would like to work on them, making your highest priority dream number one. Remember, you are not a supergirl who can fulfill all of her dreams at once. Many people never reach any of their goals because the number of goals they have set overwhelm them before they even get started. They use up their energy just thinking about all their plans.

You may be able to work on several goals at once, but you would be much better off to fully accomplish one goal than to start five and never finish any of them. Be sensitive to yourself, know yourself, know what you can handle realistically. Stretch yourself, but don't stretch yourself so far that you break. Remind yourself of the very wise saying: "Life by the inch is a cinch, life by the yard is hard."

MAKE A DREAM COME TRUE

Choose your number one dream, and step by step make it come true. Let me illustrate. Let's say that you chose getting a new hair style as your first priority. You have accepted the texture, the thinness or thickness, and the natural straightness or curliness of your hair. You want to get a hair style that makes the most of your hair givens.

Step 1. *State goal in written words.*
• My goal is to get a new hair style that is best for my hair and my face shape.

Step 2. *Set up a system for information about the goal.*
• Get a manila folder and label "Hair."
• Collect articles, information, and ideas about hair styles that would work best for me.

25

Step 3. *State goal in pictures.*

• Collect pictures of hair styles I like and put into the folder labeled "Hair."

• Display favorite pictures in a visible place such as my mirror so I can see them often and be reminded of my goal.

Step 4. *State specifically step by step how to accomplish the goal, including time and date.*

• Investigate hair stylists (call Barbara and ask her who her hairstylist is since I like her style so much).

• Decide on stylist.

• Call beauty salon Tuesday afternoon and make an appointment with (name of stylist) for next Saturday, August 1, at 10:00 A.M.

TAKE THE FIRST STEP

Your goal may not be as simple as finding a new hair style, where you know every step that you need to take. Although you may know only the first step to take toward accomplishing your goal, the important thing is to *take* that step! Do something. Don't hesitate. When you take the first step, it's amazing how you are given the insight into the next step. Just get busy making your dreams come true.

ACT ON THE KNOWLEDGE THAT YOU HAVE

"BUT, I'LL DO IT TOMORROW . . ."

Is procrastination (putting things off) a problem for you? You bet it is, huh? Do you put off a class report until the last minute? Do you put off cleaning your room? Notice the kinds of things you put off doing.

You will begin to see that they all have one thing in common: They are the things you don't enjoy doing. Right? Have you noticed you never put off the things you love to do? You are not by yourself in this. Everyone seems to have this problem to a degree (and some worse than others), but procrastination will rob you of your dreams. Sometimes you have to do things you don't particularly enjoy in order to reach your goal. That's when it's most helpful to look at the overall consequences because every act has a consequence. Do you think you will be happier with yourself in class tomorrow if you stay home tonight and study for your English test or if you go shopping with your friend instead? The answer is obvious when you look at it that way, isn't it? Which activity will be more fun? Shopping, of course. Which will build greater self-esteem? Studying for your English test. Learn to ask yourself this question when you have a decision to make: After the activity is over, which of my choices will allow me to feel the best about myself? Then set a specific time to do the thing you chose to do and enjoy the feeling that comes with knowing you made the right decision. Putting an end to procrastination and beginning to make your dreams come true will build your self-esteem and give you purpose and meaning in life in a way that nothing else can.

"I JUST CAN'T WAIT UNTIL . . ."

Do you dream a lot about the future? Your thoughts go something like this: *I just can't wait until.* . . . Write them down here.

• I just can't wait until:

_____

_____

27

Are these future dreams a possibility for you? If so, hold on to them, but don't let them rob you of your present. The present, today, is the only thing that any of us are assured of, so be sure you are living fully now. Some people postpone their entire lives. They live always thinking about someday, instead of making things happen *now*. Turn your dreams into reality instead of allowing your dreams to be a cop-out on life.

After you have accomplished your number one goal, work on your number two goal. Of course, you may decide to work on several similar goals at one time. However you choose to do it, one goal at a time or several, you will sense purpose in your life as you focus on your goals and move toward them. Become what you have the potential to be.

"The Teen I Want to Be" is the Best Me— the very Best Me!

Be sure to enjoy the process of getting there.

Notes

♥ write out my goals (be *specific* !!!)

♥ don't procrastinate

Materials

♥ file folder labeled GOALS for information and pictures concerning my goals

CHAPTER THREE

the best me with my time

♥ Do you ever wonder, while you watch sports events like the Olympics on television, how the athletes have accomplished so much—how they have developed such skill? I do. Then as I think about it, I have to admit to myself that they have made some pretty tough choices concerning the use of their time. They had to say no to many good things in life in order to practice enough to reach the goals they had set for themselves. In the same way, the quality of your life is a matter of your choices.

FEELINGS DO NOT CHANGE THINGS—ACTIONS DO

YOUR GOALS DETERMINE HOW YOU USE YOUR TIME

You know what your goals are now that you have done the exercises in the previous chapter. Your goals will guide you in how to use your time. Let's go back to the hair example. Your goal is to get a new hair style, and you have an appointment Saturday morning at 10:00. Now you must plan out your time so that you can accomplish that goal. If your friend invites you to go skating Saturday morning, you will have to say no if you still want a possible dream to become a reality.

SCHEDULING YOUR DAY IN ORDER TO REACH YOUR GOALS

1. First, write down your major goal for the day and put an asterisk (*) beside it.

2. Starting with your goal, work backward, filling in activities step by step. (What are the things you need to do before the goal can be accomplished?)

3. Fill in the remainder of the day (after the goal has been planned in).

See sample on facing page.

WRITE OUT A PLAN

The most helpful item I have found to help me manage my time is a calendar/organizer notebook. Being a model means not being late for appointments and shows because being late a few times means no more bookings. To avoid such a situation, I used a notebook to organize my modeling schedule and other areas of my life too. I developed a system that enabled me to keep up with a lot of things in spite of my very busy life. As others became interested in my ability to do this, I began teaching a time management seminar called "Running the Race." The calendar/organizer book is available for purchase. You may want to order one of them to help you organize your life and manage your time better. (An order blank is in the back of the book on page 192.)

Alan Lakein says in *How to Get Control of Your Time and Your Life* that your time *is* your life. Use that time wisely. When you make the wrong choices with your hours and minutes, your self-esteem suffers because you haven't done what you should. Remember, if you waste your time, you are wasting your life.

Decide what you want to do and write out a plan to do it. Focus on that goal. Put action behind your plan, and watch your dreams come true!

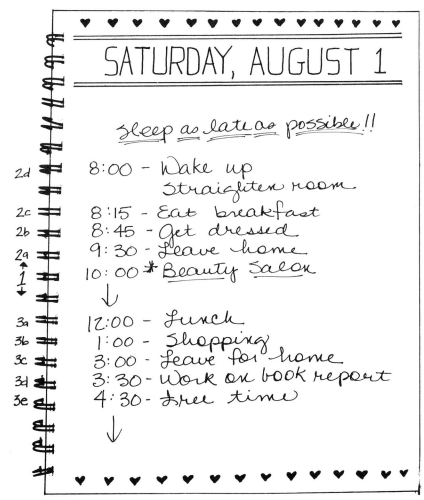

SATURDAY, AUGUST 1

sleep as late as possible!!

2d — 8:00 - Wake up
    Straighten room
2c — 8:15 - Eat breakfast
2b — 8:45 - Get dressed
2a — 9:30 - Leave home
1 — 10:00 * Beauty Salon
        ↓
3a — 12:00 - Lunch
3b — 1:00 - Shopping
3c — 3:00 - Leave for home
3d — 3:30 - Work on book report
3e — 4:30 - Free time
        ↓

Work backward, step by step from the goal.

Fill in remainder of the day after the goal.

This example applies to anything you want to accomplish in your life—whether it's getting a homework project finished on time or learning to play tennis.

Notes

♥ plan my time so that I can reach my goals

Materials

♥ calendar/organizer

CHAPTER FOUR

the best me with money

♥ What are the things you dream about having? Are they possible or impossible dreams? Believe it or not, the same principles that apply to setting your goals and managing your time apply to managing your money. First, it's a matter of what is possible for you, and then it's a matter of choices. You can't do everything, nor can you have everything. Just as you can spend your time wisely or unwisely, you can spend your money wisely or unwisely.

You are probably thinking, *Money? Who has money?* You would be shocked, I'm sure, if you knew how much money has gone through your hands. Keep a record of the money you receive or earn, regardless of how little you think it is. It adds up! You will probably be in for some surprises, too, as to how you use your money.

ALLOWANCE

Many teens say that their biggest hassles with their parents are over money. One girl told me about the fight she had with her mom over two pairs of $45 designer jeans. Have you ever done something similar?

An allowance would have prevented this problem. If she had received an allowance, including a separate clothing allowance, she would have had to make the decision as to whether she wanted to spend $90 of her total Fall/Winter clothing budget on two pairs of jeans. Get the picture?

My daughter Jodi has been on an allowance since she was very young. In her middle grammar school years, she started getting a clothing allowance in addition to her weekly allowance. I did not give her the money for her clothes, but I told her how much she had to spend. She worked out her wardrobe chart (see page 137), planned her shopping list, and worked hard to find good buys so she could get the clothes she needed and wanted with the amount of money she had to spend. This has been an invaluable lesson to her. Why not share this idea about a clothing allowance with your mom. She might like to give it a try with you.

MAKING MONEY

Money may be tight in your family, with little left for you. Instead of allowing self-pity to creep in, use your energy to come up with creative ways to make some spending money. Here are a few suggestions: (1) baby-sit; (2) make breads, cakes, cookies, and pies to sell; (3) make crafts to sell at bazaars; or (4) get a part-time job at a local mall or shopping center.

One great program for young people is sponsored by Chick-fil-A (a national fast-food chain). Truett Cathy, founder, owner, and president, is dedicated to helping young people achieve their goals by providing the opportunity for work and the opportunity to further their education at the college or school of their choice. If you have a Chick-fil-A close to you, you can make spending money now as well as qualify for a $1,000 scholarship. Since the program began in 1972, Chick-fil-A, Inc., has awarded over $2 million in scholarships to teen-agers like you. Having spending money now and getting a college education later may seem like impossible dreams to you, but they don't have to be. Get out the Yellow Pages and see if a Chick-fil-A is in your area.

Investigate other companies too. Many of them have excellent programs for young people. Make a dream come true. Where there is a will, there is a way!

A BUDGET

A good way to budget your money (excluding your clothing allowance) is to divide it into three parts:

1. *Giving.* Learn to be a giver early in your life. You will be enriched by developing this habit. Life seems to have a built-in principle that says, "You always get back more than you give." A rule of thumb for giving is 10 per cent of your allowance or what you earn. Giving involves not only money, but also time. Your community offers many opportunities for service. Consider working as a candy striper in your local hospital, shopping for the elderly, reading for the blind, working in the church nursery, assisting a scout troop leader, clearing weeds for a city beautiful project, teaching youngsters how to swim, or being a buddy to a disabled peer.

2. *Saving.* Learn to be a saver early in your life, even if you can save only twenty-five cents a week. Postpone or say no to some of your immediate desires so that you can save for the things that cost more than you have on a weekly basis. The rule of thumb for saving is 10 per cent.

3. *Spending.* This amount goes for the everyday necessities such as school lunches, plus extras. The rule of thumb for weekly spending

is 80 per cent. This amount will be less if you are saving for something special.

SLEEP ON IT

One of the wisest bits of advice I have ever received concerning money came to me as a young girl. When I saw something I thought I just couldn't live without, Daddy would say to me, "Mary Ann, why don't you sleep on it and see how you feel about it tomorrow?" Amazingly enough, most of the things I thought I couldn't do without didn't seem nearly as important to me the next day. Why don't you try this too?

TAKE GOOD CARE OF THE THINGS YOU HAVE

Managing your money well and taking good care of your possessions go hand in hand. According to the principle of multiplication, if you use what you have well, you will be given more. Abuse or do not use well what you have and you will lose it. In other words, if you want more money, use the money you have wisely.

It's up to you! You can make your possible dreams come true. As you choose to give up your impossible dreams and focus your energies on making your possible dreams come true, you will be well on your way to becoming the Best You. You can do it. And I believe you will.

Notes

- ♥ work out a budget
- ♥ talk to mom about a clothing allowance
- ♥ investigate ways to make some money

the best me to others

♥ Have you ever thought about what makes life worth living? It's relationships, isn't it? It's the relationship you have with the One who created you, the relationship you have with yourself, and the relationship you have with others.

Without meaningful relationships, your dreams seem unimportant. Life just doesn't seem worth the effort it takes. Think about some of the superwealthy superstars who had everything, it *seemed* . . . beauty and everything money could buy . . . yet life wasn't worth anything to them. They chose self-destruction through such things as alcohol and drugs. They had everything but the thing that counts the most—meaningful relationships.

I believe everyone has the same basic dream—to be loved and to love, to be accepted and to accept. I believe this is a possible dream.

TWO SIMPLE FORMULAS TO POPULARITY

Through years of studying everything I could find about relationships (friendships, how to get along with others, popularity, and so on) and through insights I gained in working with all kinds of people—typical adults and teen-agers as well as prisoners and addicted professionals living in a halfway house—I have found an incredibly simple formula. I have also found that people will do anything to gain love, admiration, and popularity . . . anything, that is, except the thing that works. The age-old formula, the Golden Rule, is this:

Do to other people what you would have them do to you.

> If you want them to love you,
> > YOU LOVE THEM.
>
> If you want them to talk to you,
> > YOU TALK TO THEM.
>
> If you would like them to invite you over,
> > YOU INVITE THEM OVER.

You will have made a giant leap forward in making your dreams come true, if you master this second simple formula to meaningful relationships:

Be an actor instead of a reactor.

Actor	Reactor
Talks	Talks only when talked to
Smiles	Smiles only when smiled at
Plans activities	Only attends activities

Do you want to go through life reacting to what everyone else is doing? No! Remember you are unique and special. You want to make things happen. You have dreams and goals. You want to reach for the stars! You want to have friends, be a friend, love and be loved. So be an actor (a leader) instead of a reactor (a follower).

YOUR FAMILY

Who are the most important people in your life? I ask this question in each of my workshops. Invariably, the answers are always the same: (1) Mom and Dad, (2) brothers and sisters, (3) grandparents, and (4) friends. Is that the way you would have answered? As the workshop unfolds, the teens begin to realize that although they consider their families the most important people in their lives, the home is not where they are the most loving and friendly. In fact, many times a teen-ager is the least loving and friendly with the people at home. What about you? Same answer? Why do you think it's that way? Let me ask you another question. If you treated your best friend the way you treat your sister, what would happen? You would no longer have a best friend, right?

HOME—A HAVEN OR A BATTLEFIELD?

Let's look at this situation a little more closely and see if we can figure it out, because it certainly doesn't make sense. Could it be that if you scream at your sister, she'll still be your sister, but if you scream at your best friend, she'll probably no longer be your best friend? Maybe we feel more secure with our families and take them for granted. Home should be a place where we can just be ourselves. It is, in a sense, a refuge, a place where we are loved and accepted for ourselves and for no other reason. But home should not be a place where we take out our frustrations with the world. Have you ever been mad at your teacher but took it out on your mom when you got home from school? Have you ever been mad at your friend and took it out on your little brother?

40

Sure, all of us have let our anger fly at someone else—someone we felt more secure with—but is that fair? No, I don't think so. It's important to deal with the situation or person involved as quickly as possible so you won't vent your feelings on someone else who has had no part in the conflict. (See "People Problems," page 50.)

Let's look at some specific questions related to this problem. Is the choice of a mom and dad a possible dream ___? or an impossible dream ___? Is the choice of brothers and sisters a possible dream ___? or an impossible dream ___? You had nothing to do with who your parents or who your brothers and sisters are . . . they are part of your givens. As I told you earlier, when a given is unchangeable, it is important for you to give it new meaning in your life by believing it is for your good. Acceptance is a part of this too.

Is your having the right attitude toward your family members a possible dream ___? or an impossible dream ___? You have control over your attitude, so it is a possible dream. You can't change who your mom, dad, brothers, and sisters are. You can't change their attitudes either, but you can change your attitude.

Throughout your life you will be in contact with people who have characteristics similar to those family members. Let me give you an illustration. Perhaps you have a big problem with your sister—you just can't stand her. You dream about the day you can get away from her forever. The room you two share is always a wreck because she is so messy. She never makes up her bed or picks up her clothes. She wears your clothes without asking, and worst of all, she is always hanging around you and your friends. The big day finally comes. You leave for college—a new life—and no more having to put up with your "bratty" sister. You meet your new college roommate. Wow, does she seem neat! How different this new life will be away from Sis. . . . The weeks roll by, and you can hardly believe what is happening. Guess who is wearing your blouse today without your permission? Guess whose bed is unmade and whose clothes are scattered all over the room? Guess who wants to stick to you like glue? You have probably guessed right. Your roommate! And you thought you were getting away from all that forever. As I said, invariably we end up with the same kinds of situations throughout our lives. A boss or husband may turn out to be just like dad, or a manager or teacher just like mom.

I was presenting "The Teen I Want to Be" Workshops in a major city, and a fashion editor from one of the city's newspapers asked for an interview. She was especially interested in the parts of the program concerning relationships. As I was sharing with her the illustration I just shared with you, I noticed the funniest look on her face. Suddenly, she said, "You know, my husband acts just like my mother!" To be honest, I thought she was going to say, "My husband acts just like my father." Her response was a new one on me, but I felt it proved again that we can't run away from what we consider to be problems.

Okay, if that's the case, what do you do about it?

Your home can serve as the "training ground" for learning how to relate to others. Learn to work out your relationships at home, where you are safe and secure. Then you will be prepared to go out into the world.

Jodi has two brothers, Jeff and Stephen. In the past, Jeff, the oldest brother, had the ability to get Jodi going in circles. Imagine a cat and a dog that can't get along together in the same room. The dog growls at the cat, and immediately the cat hisses, with the hair on her back standing straight up. That's exactly the kind of thing Jeff could do to Jodi, and he had great fun doing it! Of course, I could always separate them, but was that the answer? Jodi needed to learn how to deal with the situation herself. I said to her, as she was in tears one day, "Jodi, there will always be people like Jeff in your life, and there will be times I won't be around to help you, so it is important for you to learn how to handle Jeff and others like him." She did. She developed a simple strategy to solve the problem, although it took a lot of effort on her part to carry it out. She ignored him. What fun is it to pick on someone who ignores you? None, so Jeff lost interest in teasing her. They now have a wonderful relationship, and Jodi learned an invaluable lesson.

In the next section, let's look at family relationships more specifically.

YOUR PARENTS

Do you obey your parents? Yes ___ No ___

I know *obey* may sound like an old-fashioned word to you, but it is still a good one. Think through that word and the question I asked you. After all, you are old enough now to choose whether or not you will obey your parents. You may be thinking, as I have found most teen-agers do, that you cannot answer the question with either yes or no. Your answer would have to be "some of the time."

If that is your answer, how do you make the decision *when* you will obey? Do you obey when it is something you want to do and disobey when it is something you don't want to do? If that is your answer, you would be more honest with yourself to say, "No, I don't obey my parents. I do what *I* want to do."

Here's how *Webster's* defines *obey*: "(1) to follow the commands or guidance of (2) to comply with."

Many teen-agers dream of the day that they will be free to do what they want to do and no longer have to obey anyone. Is that a possible dream ___? or an impossible dream ___? It is an impossible dream. No one ever reaches that point. Now you have parents to obey; later you will have employers, the government, or others to obey.

If you have a good reason for not wanting to obey your parents in a particular situation, then you need to think the problem through and discuss it openly with your parents. Tell them how you feel and why, and what you would like to do. Communication is the key. If your parents still insist, after you've been honest with them, you would be wise to obey unless it violates a moral or spiritual law. Remind yourself that your parents are probably much wiser than you. Since they have already been through the teen years and many of their adult years, parents often see things that you can't possibly see at the time. Decide to trust them, even if you don't understand where they are coming from. You will grow in character.

Do you show respect to your parents? Yes ___ No ___

Years ago, when Jodi was a little toddler, I had a friend who lived next door to a family with a teen-age daughter. Many afternoons, Jodi and I would be at my friend's home for a visit at the time the teen-ager came home from school. Shortly thereafter we would hear her screaming at her mother. She would go on and on. This same scene occurred repeatedly.

The relationship between that mother and daughter really affected me. (I would almost get a sick feeling when I heard the screaming.) My gaze would fall on Jodi, my precious Jodi. I had dreamed about having a daughter since I was a little girl, and my dream had come true. I had a beautiful little dark-haired girl with big brown eyes and a bubbly, loving personality. I would think, *Will she grow into a teen-age girl and scream at me that way someday? This little girl I love so much, who throws her arms around me and covers me with sticky kisses. Will she scream at me like that?* Right then and there I determined that I would never have that kind of relationship with my daughter if I could keep from it.

I desired a relationship based on respect, one in which I would respect Jodi as a valuable person with dignity and expect that same attitude from her toward me. As a result of that decision, I have encouraged Jodi to be free to say anything she wants to me. But it must be done with respect! For instance, she will say to me "Mom, that really hurt my feelings when you _____ ," rather than scream at me about how mad I made her. When she shares her feelings with me openly and honestly, we can discuss it. We have had many wonderful times together as we have both been willing to listen to each other and work out the rough places. I, too, have chosen to be free with Jodi and share with her in a nonthreatening way what is going on within me when it involves her. Communication opens the door to the other person. Angry shouting or silence closes the door.

Do you, year by year, assume more responsibility in your home?
Yes ___ No ___

Independence is earned, and the way you earn it is to show that you are a responsible person. Do you do more or less around your home now that you are a teen-ager? It is so easy to get slack in the things you do at home because of all the demands made by school and friends. For instance, in grade school you may have consistently made your bed, but as you have gotten older and had more activities in your life, you rush out many mornings without making your bed. Don't neglect your routine duties. Take responsibility for some things around the house. Become a dependable person. Then when the time comes for you to begin driving, dating, and going off to school, your parents will know that you are ready. By your actions, show that you have earned the right to independence rather than demand your independence.

Do you look for ways to help your family have more fun?
Yes ___ No ___

Have you ever considered the fact that your family could have lots of fun together? Why not get to know each family member better? Play a guessing game at the dinner table. Guess each person's favorite meal, favorite ice cream, favorite restaurant, or favorite color. Add to the list of favorites. Plan a picnic outing for your family. Be responsible for every detail, and see how creative you can be in what you include in the picnic basket. Or put a puzzle together on a cold winter's night. Ask your mom and dad about their teen years. You are creating memories that will be precious to you.

Do you always make sure that your parents know your close friends?
Yes ___ No ___

Most likely you do. Your close friends are probably at your home often, and you are probably at their homes often. As parents, Joe and I always wanted to know Jeff's, Stephen's, and Jodi's close friends as well as their close friends' parents. We also liked to know their phone numbers and where they lived in case we needed to get in touch with the children while they were there. Joe and I feel our lives have been enriched by getting to know and becoming friends with our children's friends and parents.

Whom do you go to for advice? _____

I have often found in working with teen-agers that the ones with serious problems usually go to other teen-agers for counsel or advice.

46

And to make matters more complicated, they often go to friends whose lives are as messed up as theirs or maybe even more so. If your friends can't work out their own problems, how do you think they can solve yours? Be very careful about selecting the person you share your problems with. Of course I am not saying *not* to share things with your close friends. That's one of the qualities of a close friendship. Just be wise.

The best person you can choose for a counselor/advisor is your mom (or your dad). They love you. They have known you since you were born, and they have your best interests at heart (even if they don't always know how to show it). Learn to confide in them. You may be thinking, *You don't know my mom.* No, I don't, but in all probability she wants you to have confidence in her and confide in her even if she doesn't know how to develop that kind of relationship with you. You may have to take the initiative with her. Go to her and tell her that you need to be able to talk confidentially with her. These years are tough and you need all the support you can get. You can remind her that if you can't talk to her you will have to confide in a friend and you would rather not. Once you begin this kind of relationship, your life will be greatly enriched.

Jodi knows that I am behind her 100 per cent. Her world may fall apart, but her mom will still be there cheering for her and believing in her. She knows that next to her dad, she is my best friend. This relationship has been cemented and bonded through many tears as well as joys. You deserve someone on your team too!

YOUR BROTHERS AND SISTERS

What about brothers and sisters (if you have any)? Remember I said earlier, the real test of learning how to get along with others is learning how to get along with your family members. It is worth every effort you can make to learn to live with them in a meaningful way. Throughout your life you will meet people with characteristics similar to those of family members. The earlier you learn to get along well at home, the less you will have to work at learning how to relate to others in your larger world. Don't forget this: Friends come and go, but your family is your family forever.

I had a "best friend" from the eighth through the twelfth grades. We did everything together. She lived several blocks from our high school, while I lived about twelve miles away and rode a school bus. Her home became my home away from home. We both played in the band and participated in lots of extracurricular activities. When an activity ended late in the evening, I would stay overnight at her house so my parents would not have to drive the round trip for me. Graduation came, and we went our separate ways. She went away to college, married shortly before finishing, and moved across the United States. I have seen her once since her marriage, and that was years ago.

My two sisters and I were not as close during my teen years as my best friend and I were, but guess who I still see often? Yes, my sisters. The three of us have families of our own, but we still get together during holidays and special occasions. We take each other out for birthday celebrations, and we lend support to each other as well as to each other's families. I have lost touch with my high-school best friend, but the relationship with my sisters grows richer each year.

What is your relationship like with your brothers and sisters? Do you argue with them most of the time you are together? Yes ___ No ___

Don't get into the habit of trying to pick a fight with your brothers and sisters. That's not to say that you should never have disagreements, however. Disagreements are a part of relating with other people, and it is unhealthy to keep all of your thoughts and feelings inside. In my work with women prisoners and drug-addicted and alcoholic patients, I saw that they all had an underlying problem—one of not knowing how to communicate with others. Learn to express yourself with parents, brothers, sisters, and everyone else. Claim your thoughts and feelings; state what they are, but don't blame others. The arguments start when you blame them instead of telling them how you feel.

Which do you do the most, criticize your brothers and sisters or compliment them? _____

No one likes to be criticized, but everyone likes to be complimented. Of course, your compliments must be sincere. You may be surprised at the positive effects of your words.

Do you show the same good manners to your brothers and sisters that you do to your friends? Yes ___ No ___

When asking them to do something, do you ask with a "please" in the sentence or do you make demands? Be as courteous to your family as you are to your friends.

Do you ever do anything special for your brothers and sisters?
Yes ___ No ___

Maybe they don't deserve it. You may be thinking, *That little bratty brother of mine doesn't deserve a thing.* Do something special for him anyway! It will do wonders for you and might even help him. Anyone can be nice to someone who is always nice in return. It's being nice to the tough ones, like your little brother, that strengthens you and refines your character.

PEOPLE PROBLEMS

Resolving Your Conflicts

This puts the responsibility squarely on you, and you are the only one who can do anything about your situation. Let me show you how you could apply the four steps to solving a problem or conflict.

When you have a problem with someone, what do you think about all of the time? More than likely, that person and that problem. You play the problem over and over in your mind like a stuck record. You think about what you should have done, how you dislike the person, and what you will do to get even. Think back on the times you have done this. It didn't make you feel better—and it didn't solve the problem. The funny thing is that the person with whom you are in conflict may be totally unaware of any problem and be happily going on with life while you are destroying yours. Nothing is worth your hurting yourself in this way. Therefore, determine to resolve your conflicts with others to the very best of your ability. You don't have time for conflicts! Keep your thoughts free to dream your dreams, work on your goals, and enjoy your friends and loved ones.

I am very angry with Anne.	Step 1. *Who.*	Write down who you are having a conflict with.
She ignored me and did not speak to me today in the cafeteria.	Step 2. *Why.*	Write down exactly why you are hurt or angry or whatever with the person.
I would like for her to have smiled at me and spoken to me . . . to have acknowledged me as a person.	Step 3. *What you wanted.*	Write down exactly what you wanted or what you would have liked for the other person to have done.
Tomorrow I will make a point to speak to Anne in a warm and friendly way and not wait for her to speak to me. In fact, she might have been in deep thought about something and not have seen me.	Step 4. *The golden rule.*	Do to or for the person what you would have liked for the person to have done to or for you.

50

THE BEST ME TO OTHERS

FRIENDS

There are different levels of friendship: close friends, casual friends, and acquaintances. Knowing the level of friendship you have with a person is important. Have you ever told someone a secret and she told others? Do you have friends who always accept your invitations but never invite you to do anything with them? All of us know the pain of having misjudged a relationship. The important thing is what we learn from the experience.

Most people have many casual friendships and a few close ones. Everyone cannot be a close friend to you because developing a relationship takes a lot of time and effort. Close friends accept each other, both their good and not-so-good qualities. They are friends during the down times as well as the up times. Close friends are people with whom you have much in common.

Have you ever heard the old sayings: "You are judged by the company you keep" and "Birds of a feather flock together"? There is a lot of truth in these adages. Unless people have some common area of interest, they do not become close friends. You may start a relationship with someone based on your desire to help and that's okay. It is admirable to want to help others, but if you find you are spending all of your time with that person, you may be enjoying that relationship more than you want to admit. Choose your close friends from those who share your values. We become like those we stay around.

In close friendships there should be almost equal give and take. Some people only know how to be takers, while others only know how to be givers. Neither quality alone makes for a good relationship. The relationship should be balanced. Now that certainly doesn't mean that you are going to keep score, that you are going to call her only when she has called you, or that if she spends five dollars on your birthday, you are

51

going to spend exactly five dollars on her birthday. No! Keeping score kills a relationship. What you give to each other may not be the same and what you receive from each other may not be the same, but you will share the same goals and commitment to each other. One of the most painful times in my life was when I had to accept the fact that someone that I wanted a close friendship with did not want one with me. But the acceptance of that fact freed me from constantly being hurt and allowed me to concentrate on the people in my life who did want to be close friends.

Casual friends and acquaintances make up all the many other people in your life. As time goes by, some of those people will become closer friends, but most will remain in the larger circle of your life. Never underestimate the importance of any person in your life, though. You never know the significant part an individual may someday play in your life or vice versa. My life has been enriched many times by people I just happened to meet. In fact, this book's being published by Oliver-Nelson is the result of a casual friendship made fifteen years ago with a missionary at a seminar. I never forgot him, and he never forgot me. I hope I too have enriched others' lives. Every encounter and meeting in your life is of tremendous importance.

DATING

Dating is very much a part of this time in your life whether you have actually begun to date or whether you just dream about it. Dating can be fun or devastating or a mixture of both. You learn how to relate meaningfully to the opposite sex just as you have learned how to have meaningful relationships with other girls. It's a sign of maturity when you can view dating as another facet of friendship. As you develop those friendships, you'll discover what you like in guys; therefore, dating ultimately helps you make a wise choice in your selection of a husband.

Yes, dating can be a painful time. Imagine that the junior-senior prom is coming up. All of your friends have been invited, but you have not. You are hurt badly, and you wonder, *What is wrong with me?* You may even be tempted to get a friend to set you up with someone you really don't care for, just to keep from feeling left out. Don't compromise your standards. Being without a date happens to everyone at one time or another. Next year you may have more invitations than you can accept while your friends sit at home.

Try to be relaxed about it all. Many girls are so uptight over whether or not they will be asked for a date that boys are scared off. So take it easy. Try to have the attitude that if you are asked for a date, it's OK, and if you are not, it's OK. Instead of concentrating on getting boys to ask you out, concentrate on becoming all you can be both inside and out. Something about vibrant, growing persons causes other people, both male and female, to want to be around them. Think about the most well-liked people you know. They are fun to be with, and they have varied interests. They are at peace with themselves because they like themselves. They are not trying to find their security in others.

Before you go on your next date, why not think about a set of dating rules? Write down your values, what you will or will not do on a date. Your list should include information on what type of boy you will date, places you will go, activities you will be involved in and activities you will not accept such as smoking, drinking, taking drugs, and getting involved physically. Once your list is completed, you're ready to go on that date. You've determined some things in your heart, and your decisions were made before you walked out the door. Keeping true to them will help you stay out of situations you don't want to be in.

My dating standards:

_____

_____

_____

_____

_____

_____

_____

_____

_____

_____

I think it's a good idea to show your list of standards to your parents. Ask them to go over the list with you and make any changes they do not agree with. Ask them to add to it in any way they see fit (I wish I could hear your reaction right now). I offer this same suggestion in "The Teen I Want to Be" Workshops. The responses from the girls indicate they think I may be a little crazy. Do you? I will ask you the same question that I ask them. As a result of your writing out your dating standards and discussing them with your parents, do you think your parents will be more strict on you or have more confidence in you? All of the workshop participants answer unanimously, "Have more confidence in me."

Before Jodi began to date she wrote out her dating standards. She then asked her dad to take her out on a "date." (I wasn't invited.) They got all dressed up, and he took her to one of the nicest restaurants in Atlanta. While they were there, she shared with him that she thought it was getting close to time for her to begin dating. She said she had done a lot of thinking about it and wanted him to know what she expected of herself and the guys she dated. Needless to say, her dad was overjoyed with the decisions she had made. I can assure you that we felt she had shown a great deal of maturity. Indeed, she was ready to begin dating if she chose to.

Jodi said to me one day, "Mom, it was easy to stick to my dating standards in high school. I wasn't even tempted to do otherwise, but it has been much harder in college with all of the social activities. I am so thankful that I made those decisions in high school and stuck to them. It has kept me from dating really cute guys whose standards were much lower than mine, guys that I knew in my heart I shouldn't get involved with."

There will come a time when you are asked out by a guy you do not

54

want to go out with. How will you handle it? The first time he asks you, you will probably say you are busy, right? The second time he asks you, you will probably say the same thing, right? He may be a very persistent guy, and you know you can't keep making up excuses forever. So what should you do? In this case honesty is probably the best policy. In a very kind way, tell him that you want to continue your friendship with him as it is, but you would rather not go out with him. Do not feel pressured into dating anyone that you do not want to go out with or anyone your parents disapprove of. Be sure that you reject the date instead of the person. Don't make *him* feel rejected. It may have taken a lot of courage for him to ask you out the first time and even more the second and third times.

Boys are just as unsure of themselves as girls are. My friend's eighth-grade son called a girl in his class twenty times before he had the courage to stay on the line and talk to her! Now imagine if she had said, "You dummy, don't ever call me again!" He might have never called another girl for the rest of his life. So girls, don't go if you don't want to, but show a little mercy in refusing.

Every girl needs to learn to say one little word, "No." Many girls get involved with guys in ways they never intended to because they feel intimidated and do not have the courage to say no. Fear of being by ourselves and the need for acceptance and love are areas that we all need to face in our lives. Be willing to be alone, if necessary, when the other alternative is going against your own standards (remember your list). You may stand out from the crowd and seem different, but you won't regret it. You will have your own self-respect as well as that of others, even though they may be making fun of you at the time. Don't do anything that will lower your opinion of yourself—the wonderful person of great value that you are.

When should you begin dating? I don't think there is a set time. The time to begin is obviously influenced by your parents' consent, the boy asking you out, and your wanting to date him. Remember, dating should be a fun part of your teen years. It's a means of making friends with many different guys. Don't get hung up on marriage and wonder if every boy who asks you out is "Mr. Right," your future husband. Relax. Don't rush it. Don't settle for less than your best!

LIFE'S MOST IMPORTANT SKILLS

Meaningful relationships truly are what gives life purpose and excitement. Of all the skills you learn in life, these will be the most beneficial. Your dream possibilities are in direct proportion to how you relate to the One who created you, to yourself, and to others.

Notes

- ♥ treat others the way I want to be treated
- ♥ become more responsible
- ♥ show appreciation & love to the most important people in my life
- ♥ be friendly
- ♥ don't be afraid to "stand alone" if necessary
- ♥ write out my dating standards

I ♥ you

CHAPTER SIX

the best me size

♥ Have you ever observed people as they go through a cafeteria line? Think about the food choices they make. You will get some insight into why some people are overweight, some are too thin, and some are average weight. It takes all the mystery out of weight. Very few people have a physical problem that makes them either overweight or underweight. They simply eat more calories than their bodies burn and they store the excess as fat, or they eat fewer calories than their bodies need and the fat is robbed from their bodies to burn for energy. Let's get back to the cafeteria line. Imagine an overweight person, a thin person, and an average weight person going through the line. All three are given five choices. What foods do you think each would choose?

Five Food Choices

Miss Overweight	Miss Underweight	Miss Averageweight
1.	1.	1.
2.	2.	2.
3.	3.	3.
4.	4.	4.
5.	5.	5.

EMOTIONAL REASONS FOR EATING

The reasons you eat or do not eat are much more complex than calories. One reason for *not* wanting to eat is that we live in a society that worships beauty in the female. Our particular time in history equates thinness with beauty, but this has not always been so. Other periods of history have valued full-bodied females. If you don't believe me, go to the museum and look at the old masters' paintings. On the other hand, one reason *for* eating is that it is tied closely to love. Food is one of the most important aspects of life. We first experienced love when our mothers held us closely and fed us. When we combine these two aspects (being thin to gain acceptance and eating to feel loved), we girls have an obvious problem. Both areas need to be explored in terms of your own life.

When do you eat? Do you eat only at mealtimes, or do you snack all day long? Do you eat to maintain your body, or do you eat for other reasons? (There was a period in my life when I felt, on an unconscious level, that eating a piece of cheesecake was a way of rewarding or loving myself—look out pounds.) On the other hand, do you not eat meals? Do you pride yourself in being able to do without food?

ANOREXIA NERVOSA

Let me give you two examples of girls who considered their weight a problem. My first example deals with a disease that has become prevalent in today's world—anorexia nervosa. Because I felt information on anorexia should be included in the subject of weight control, I asked a friend of mine to tell her daughter Sally's story.

"At age ten, for the very first time in Sally's life, she began to have a chunky shape. She was not fat, just not as slender as was normal for her. Something caused Sally to be dissatisfied enough with her physical appearance to do something about it. She began to diet at age twelve. Sally did not count calories, she simply cut out afternoon snacks. She ate regular meals and with just her normal routine of soccer and sports, she lost eight pounds, grew two inches in height and, in cooperation with the process of puberty, she began to have a small waist. For the first time in three years she received affirmation about her body and how great she looked—much of it expressed to her in terms of "My, you have lost weight. You look wonderful."

"Sally was not into rigorous dieting. How then, suddenly, did this sensible approach go haywire and become a compulsive, irrational, relentless pursuit of being thin?

"Normal dieting for Sally became abnormal. Why? I have learned that when this happens, nearly always some major change in a young girl's life has been the catalyst. It is a 'crisis,' real or imagined. This can be the loss of a loved one, a move to a new town, or something equally stressful. In my daughter's case, it was the impending change to a new high school. Her dieting began just before Christmas the year preceding her transfer. Her goal was to get in shape for her new school. The affirmation she received for her weight loss was nonstop. As the days drew nearer for school to start, I think she also began to feel scared, threatened, and alone.

"Nearly every ad on TV preaches that if you are beautiful or thin enough, you will be popular and everyone will love you. Above anything else, Sally wanted to look good at her new school. If being slender is a measure of beauty, then losing a pound or two more should be that much better. Actually the weight loss only touches the surface of what was truly going on inside Sally. She probably wasn't even aware of her inner struggle. Sally simply saw her pounds coming off.

"The weight loss was acceptable to us as parents until just before school started. It was then an observable change became apparent in Sally's personality. She began to be driven to exercise. She cut eating normal meals to minimal amounts. Nothing was allowed to interfere with her plans to exercise, which took more and more time each day. Her normal dieting had become compulsive behavior which was 'driven.' She resorted to pleading, anger, manipulation, and desperation to achieve the exercise/diet program she set for herself.

"Sally affected the whole family by her behavior in a short time, because so much of what we do with others involves eating! Sally had no time to eat or be sociable because her regime took more and more time every day. If she did one level of exercise one day, the following day she did more.

"It is helpful to remember that it is normal for teen-agers to feel terrible about themselves some of the time. Most teen-agers' diet is one of feast/famine. The big difference in losing weight and becoming anorexic is in degree, and in what is actually going on inside. Weight loss is only a symptom, not the problem. Because such anger, conflict, and stress were apparent, my husband sought counsel from a psychologist long before Sally's weight had dropped very much. It dropped fifteen more pounds during counseling. I did not know how to help my daughter. She did not want my help. She denied she had a problem, and she resisted counseling. Because we believed counseling was essential for healing and wholeness, we took Sally and we went ourselves.

"An anorexic girl must be carefully led to examine her mind set that says to her that she is only valuable if she is beautiful . . . beauty earmarked by being thin. She must see her own worth as a person and get to know who she is, what she wants from life, what her gifts and abilities are, what makes her unique. She must deal eventually with how she feels about herself and acknowledge her givens. She must come to grips with those things about herself that are unchangeable, her height, her bone structure, her temperament. It may be interesting to note at this point that anorexic girls are usually attractive (even pretty), very intelligent, seldom more than ten pounds overweight, and come from affluent, highly motivated, successful families.

"I have learned as an anorexic's mother that I had a lot to do with my own daughter's illness and recovery. There were many things that were not right in our family. We had, as a mother and father, failed to create a climate for Sally to feel free to be herself. It takes real courage for both the teen-ager and the parents as they look some tough facts in the face, decide to deal with them, and love and forgive one another. We had to get to know one another. We had to really listen to Sally, and she had to be willing to reveal herself. It takes a long time for a noncommunicating relationship to become open. None of this will take place except in a climate of love, forgiveness, and confession.

"How has this experience with anorexia turned out? Sally has gone from a thirteen year old at slightly over five feet in height and a low of 68 pounds to a seventeen year old who is about five-feet-two inches and weighs a healthy 110 pounds. She has accepted this as a realistic weight for her. She has a given in her hips and thighs that she wishes she could change. She has accepted it, though, and dresses to make that area look the best it can.

"Sally is OK, and I mean that in the fullest sense. She feels good about herself inside, and her weight can vary. It is OK. She is able to take the everyday storms of life for what they are—just storms—and she remains intact and OK. Sally has a natural tendency to excel (so do I). I think one thing we have learned over the past four years is that we are both OK if we do not excel. Our worth is not dependent on what we do. I am valuable just the way I am, and she is too. I do not have to be better than anyone else.

"How are we different today as a family? I think we have failed successfully! About five months after Sally's illness began, I remember our counselor asking me, 'Do you feel like a failure?' I left his office that day and spent an hour alone in my car thinking about my answer. Yes, I had 'failed' as Sally's mother. The daughter my parenting produced was not equipped to deal with life as it is. She was starving herself to death.

"I had failed but was not a failure. Our family was failing but did not fail. We were willing to learn, to change. We have learned about our weaknesses and our strengths. Sally still struggles with negative feelings (so do I). The healthy thing is that she talks about them and doesn't let her bad feelings control her. She doesn't have to be thin to be a valuable, likable person anymore."

OVERWEIGHT

The second example is given by permission from my daughter Jodi. Probably the most painful time in Jodi's life was her preteen and early teen years. During her sixth-, seventh-, and eighth-grade years, Jodi was a little overweight (which is not unusual for a girl at that time of her life because her body is going through so many changes). It was a trying time for me as her mother too! I knew the pain it caused her, and I knew how much happier and healthier she would be if she lost the extra ten to fifteen pounds. I felt that I had to be very cautious, though, not to make her feel that I would love her more if she were thinner. Of course, my love for her had nothing to do with how much she weighed but I feared because I was a fashion model, she would feel unloved unless she were thin.

I can still see the pain and disappointment on her face as she tried to get into pair after pair of jeans in the fitting room as we shopped one day. She handled it beautifully on the outside, but I knew she was dying on the inside. I tried to encourage her and find ways of making our shopping trip fun, but her disappointment and guilt lingered all afternoon.

We had tried a number of diets for Jodi with no success. Then I had a new brainstorm. We would both join a diet program and lose weight together. I really didn't need to lose weight (which I'm sure Jodi knew) but I thought that might be the answer for her. Well, you can guess the results. It didn't work! You can't make another person lose weight (or gain weight). Jodi was aware of what she needed to do, but she just wasn't able, it seemed, to do it. She faced too many temptations from too many different places.

Finally, one day something happened within Jodi. She decided she was going to lose weight. The decision came about after an unhappy experience. When she got on the school bus one day, she overheard two of her classmates whispering. She didn't know what they were saying, but she thought they were talking about her weight. Crushed, she came home and cried. Even though the experience was painful, it caused her to start thinking about her weight. She decided the weight caused her too many problems, kept her body out of shape, and generally just wasn't worth it. She had had enough! She was going to lose her weight. Once she set her mind on her goal, she didn't stop until she had lost the desired amount. Somedays she overate, but she didn't give up. She started new the next day. Her determination and will power never faltered.

Jodi has maintained her ideal weight for so long now that we can hardly believe she was ever overweight. She hasn't regained any weight because she totally changed her way of eating, and that didn't stop when she reached her ideal weight.

Those few painful years for Jodi caused her to develop a sensitivity to other people's needs. It gave a beautiful, caring dimension to her personality. She has encouraged and helped countless young girls to lose weight and to believe in themselves. Perhaps she can help you too.

JODI'S WEIGHT CONTROL TIPS

Do not deprive yourself of food. Crash diets are out! If you get hungry enough, you will eat no matter how much you want to lose weight. Instead of thinking in terms of losing weight, think in terms of eating nutritiously.

Take the guesswork out. The following steps will help you determine your ideal weight and plan to achieve it. You need to know:

Step 1. *Your ideal weight.*

Height	Small Frame	Medium Frame	Large Frame
5′	89–97	94–106	102–118
5′1″	92–100	97–109	105–121
5′2″	95–112	100–113	108–125
5′3″	98–106	103–117	112–129
5′4″	101–110	107–122	116–133
5′5″	105–114	111–126	120–137
5′6″	109–118	115–130	124–141
5′7″	113–122	119–134	128–145
5′8″	117–127	123–138	132–150
5′9″	121–131	127–142	134–153
5′10″	125–135	131–146	140–160

Weights are average for a fifteen-year-old girl. For each inch of height over five ten, add two to four pounds.

Step 2. *The number of pounds you need to lose.*

Step 3. *The number of calories you need to eliminate.*

It takes a reduction of 3,500 calories to lose 1 pound (3,500 calories times number of pounds you want to lose equals the number of calories you must eliminate). Let's look at an example. Suppose you wanted to lose five pounds. Multiply 3,500 by 5 pounds, and you'll get 17,500 calories. You should cut back about 500 calories a day from the number of calories it takes to keep you at your ideal weight. So divide 17,500 by 500 to determine how many days it will take you to reach your goal (which would be 35 days to lose 5 pounds). Most people go on crash diets and cut back too drastically on their food intake. This is a very unhealthy practice.

Step 4. *How many calories you eat each day.*

Determine the calorie count for each item of food you eat, record it, and add up the calories for the day.

Step 5. *The "no" foods.*

These foods are no-no's whether or not you want to lose weight:

- NO sugar (check labels on everything)
- NO refined flour products
- NO fried foods
- NO gravies and sauces

- NO animal or hydrogenated fat
- NO added salt

Step 6. *The "yes" foods.*

- YES vegetables, raw or steamed
- YES fruit, preferably raw
- YES whole grain products
- YES milk products, low-fat content milk, cheese, cottage cheese, plain yogurt
- YES lean meats—fish, poultry, small amount of beef
- YES bulk—high fiber fruits and vegetables, include skin of fruits and vegetables when possible
- YES 1 teaspoon vegetable oil per day (corn, safflower, sunflower, wheat germ, olive, or soybean) in margarine or a salad dressing
- TAKE a multi-vitamin and mineral tablet per day
- DRINK six to eight glasses of water per day

Step 7. *How much you weigh each morning before breakfast.*

Keep a record of your weight. You may show a weight increase, due to water retention, when you have not actually gained weight, but if the extra pound or pounds show up three mornings in a row, you need to cut back on your calories.

KEEP MOTIVATED

For motivation, place a picture of yourself at your ideal weight in a spot where you can see it often. If you do not have a picture of yourself, find a picture of someone who is approximately the size you are working toward. Remember to focus on changing your eating habits, rather than on depriving yourself of food!

You may have never had the struggles that either Jodi or Sally had. Just by the blessings of nature you may have been able to "pig out" on junk food, yet remain the ideal weight for your height and bone structure. Don't take that blessing for granted! Sooner or later your body will be affected by your eating incorrectly. It will affect you in one or more of the following ways—weight, stamina, complexion, and general overall health.

Eat to be fit. Think about your weight in a completely different way. The size of your body has nothing to do with your worth as a person. Because you are of tremendous value and worth, decide to do everything you can to take care of your body.

Forget about dieting. Don't *diet.* Eat correctly now and for the rest of your life. If you are overweight and you eat correctly, you will lose weight. If you are too thin and you eat correctly, you will gain weight. If you are average weight and eat correctly, junk foods will be cut to a minimum. Diets can be very harmful to your body because they deprive it of important nutrients as well as throw your system out of balance. Crash dieting only leads to your feeling starved and weak (and probably irritable). You are now set up to break the diet and then feel disappointed and angry with yourself. Learn all you can about your body and how it functions. Study the Basic Four food groups. Make sure you eat something from each of these groups daily.

Drink plenty of water. Drink eight glasses every day in order to wash the toxic poisons from your system and to hydrate your skin from within.

The more you know about nutrition, the better equipped you will be to withstand the many temptations around you. It won't be a life or death matter in most cases if you splurge occasionally and eat junk food, but try to keep it to a minimum. Remember that you are learning to make the right choices for yourself.

♥ 4 Basic Foods ♥

Bread + cereal group ♥

Meat group ♥

♥ Fruit + Vegetable group

♥ Milk group

I. *Bread and cereal group.* Do not eliminate bread from your life in order to lose weight. You need to replace those empty refined products. Eat whole grain breads and cereals. They give you a lot of staying power. Foods from this group produce energy, help break down food, and help to use other nutrients.

II. *Meat group.* Keep red meat to a minimum. Choose from the fish and poultry categories as much as possible. This food group supplies protein for building and repairing the body and helps build red blood cells.

III. *Fruit and vegetable group.* Eat plenty of fresh fruits and vegetables! Eat as many raw as you can, and eat the skin if possible. If you are cutting back on calories, keep a small plastic bag of celery and carrot sticks with you so you won't be tempted to eat junk food snacks. If vegetables are eaten raw or steamed and not seasoned with fat, you can eat all you want! These foods promote growth, keep the skin, bones, teeth, gums, and walls of the blood vessels strong and healthy, and help the body resist infection.

IV. *Milk group.* If you are cutting back on calories, drink skim milk and eat low-fat milk products. This group provides a good source of calcium and protein, builds strong bones and teeth, helps blood to clot, is important in the work of nerves and muscles, helps keep skin and eyes in good condition, reduces fatigue, and promotes relaxation and sleep.

68

Notes

- ♥ determine my ideal weight
- ♥ eat foods that are good for me!!

LOVE YOUR BODY

Learn to love your body too much to abuse it by giving in to certain peer pressures. Smoking, drinking alcoholic beverages, and using drugs are absolutely off limits to you if you love yourself

Love your body by keeping in tune to its needs. Learn to know the difference between being hungry for food or being hungry for emotional reasons. Eat the foods that will ensure your being your best self!

CHAPTER SEVEN

the best me shape

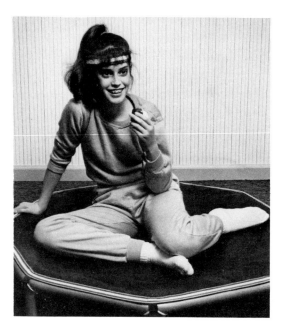

♥ Do you know that even a thin body can be out of shape? What is yours like? In panties and bra, stand in front of a full-length mirror and analyze your figure, front and back. Check the following areas.

Tummy	☒ flat	☐ protruding
Thighs	☐ smooth and shapely	☐ flabby
Buttocks	☒ firm and trim	☐ falling
Back	☒ straight	☐ stooped
Shoulders	☒ upright	☐ slumped
Chin	☒ firm	☐ sagging, double chin
Head	☐ erect	☒ forward

70

If you are the right weight for your height and bone structure but have sags, bags, and no energy, then you definitely need exercise. If your hands and feet are usually cold and you get breathless easily, you need to get your body moving! It takes a combination of exercise and diet to make you physically fit.

BENEFITS OF EXERCISE

The number one bonus of exercising is the effect it has on your cardiovascular system. Vigorous exercise forces your heart, which is a muscle, to work harder and beat faster. This strengthens your heart and increases the blood flow throughout your whole body. Your lungs take in more oxygen. Every part of your body is positively affected when you exercise at the correct pace for yourself. [CAUTION! The exercises described in this chapter are for girls in normal good health. If you have a health problem or think you might have a health problem, check with your doctor before engaging in any exercise program.]

Exercise even affects your mental and emotional attitude. When you are feeling blue, instead of lying down and having a pity party, go outside and jog, play tennis, or work out vigorously and see how the clouds lift. Exercise is a great release for bottled-up emotions, and your thinking will become clearer and more rational. Physical activity is becoming an important part of mental and emotional therapy.

Another great bonus of exercise is that it suppresses your appetite! Have you ever run three or four miles? You probably weren't even slightly hungry after you finished. Besides suppressing your appetite, exercise increases the rate your body burns calories. If you have a sluggish metabolism or you eat out of boredom, get out and exercise. Get that body moving!

How Do You Feel Most of the Time?

	Yes	No
Tired	X	
Cold hands and feet		X
Shortness of breath		X
Depressed		X
Bored	X	

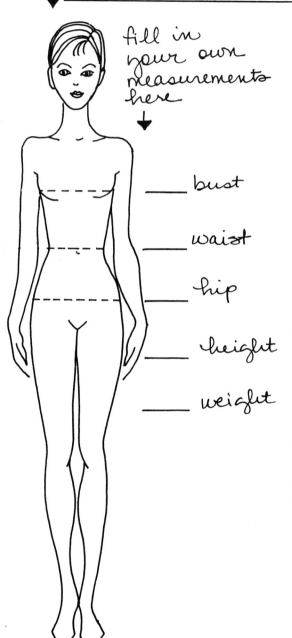

fill in
your own
measurements
here
↓

___ bust

___ waist

___ hip

___ height

___ weight

And, of course, you don't mind the fact that it tones your body, do you? Exercise stretches and strengthens the muscles all over your body, keeping the organs in place and the body in proper alignment. You become toned and firm. Bathing suit season will become a time you won't have to dread!

Have you ever noticed how much clearer your skin is when you exercise? The body rids itself of toxic poisons through the skin, the face is stimulated through increased blood to the face, and the skin is toned. Exercise is the greatest beautifying agent that I know of. It is better for your skin than the most expensive facials, and it doesn't have to cost a penny!

WORK OUT AN EXERCISE PLAN

Exercise doesn't just happen, though. Just as you must make the right food choices, you must think through, plan, and make the right exercise choices. Just as you can eat too much or too little for your optimum benefit, you can also exercise too much or too little. I have to be honest and say that I exercise too little. It's an area that I have to constantly work on. I have to tell myself the reasons that I need to make the effort. You may be like me, or you may be one of those exercise buffs who exercises more than is needed. You may be stressing your body through too much physical activity and not enough rest time. The important thing is to work *for* your body, not against it. Know the benefits of different kinds of exercises. Understand your body, and work out a plan that is best for you. There are several good books on the market to guide you in proper exercises.

72

AEROBIC EXERCISE

Aerobic exercise is exercise that sustains the heart rate for twenty to thirty minutes three times a week. If at any point you are unable to talk comfortably, the exercise is too vigorous and you need to slow down your pace.

Benefits

- Makes heart work harder and beat faster
- Increases oxygen supply by making lungs work harder

CALISTHENIC EXERCISE

Calisthenic exercises are important for the warm-up and cool-down periods in conjunction with aerobic exercise. Calisthenics are good for reshaping problem areas too.

Benefits

- Stretches and tones the body
- Strengthens muscles

For maximum benefit to your body, both aerobic and calisthenic exercises should be included in your program.

Exercise is the most fun when you can be involved with someone else in a game such as tennis or racquetball. Try to develop at least one sport that you enjoy and that gives you the aerobic benefit. You will probably need to supplement that activity with additional exercise. I believe the whole person benefits the most from exercising outdoors in the fresh air, surrounded by nature. Of course that is not always possible, so work out a program you can do indoors and alone. My favorites are jumping rope when I travel and rebounding at home.

Aerobic Activities

- Bicycling
- Dancing
- Jogging
- Jumping rope
- Race walking
- Playing racquetball, squash, or tennis
- Rebounding
- Skating
- Skiing
- Swimming

Calisthenic Activities

- Stretching and bending in exercise
- Working out with exercise equipment
- Sit-ups
- Leg lifts
- Pushups

73

Jumping rope is a lot of fun and can be done no matter what the weather or your location. (If conditions permit, you can jump outside in the fresh air!) The cost of the equipment is minimal, and you can take the rope with you anywhere. I became sold on this form of exercise about eight years ago when I read an article, "Hop, Skip and Jump to Health" by Curtis Mitchell, in *Reader's Digest.* I became a believer when I learned that Jack Baker had reported in *Research Quarterly* that "10 minutes with the rope is equal to 30 on the road." For a person who is not exactly an exercise buff, that is great news!

TIPS FOR JUMPING ROPE

- Wear jogging shoes.
- Build up gradually until you can do five hundred skips in five minutes without stopping. This will take you four to five weeks to accomplish without putting too much stress on your body.
- Jump to music to make it more fun.

My other favorite indoor exercise is rebounding. If you have a rebounder (a minitrampoline), jump on it doing the exercises to music. *Hooked on Classics* is great music for rebounding. Each segment is approximately five minutes long, so it is already timed for you. Do not jump in your sock feet because you may slip and fall. Your bare feet will give you the needed traction. Let me inject a note of caution here. With all exercises such as jumping rope and rebounding, be sure to jump using the entire bottom of your foot, not just your toes. Jumping on your toes is bad for the muscles in your legs.

An overall exercise program set to music, which incorporates both aerobic and calisthenic exercises, ensures that your whole body gets a workout. The program described here takes twenty to thirty minutes, depending on the number of repetitions you choose to do.

74

SOME IMPORTANT RULES TO FOLLOW WHEN EXERCISING

1. Always hold your stomach in tightly while exercising (think about pulling your stomach in toward your backbone).
2. Keep your back flat, and your bottom tucked under. Don't work with your lower back arched because you can easily injure this area in a swayback position.
3. Stretch out each area after you have exercised it.
4. Keep your knees loose. Don't ever lock them while doing an exercise.
5. Breathe. This may sound funny to you, but many people hold their breath while they are working out hard. Your muscles need oxygen to function well. Proper breathing will make exercising easier and more effective.
6. Don't overdo exercising. If an exercise is too painful, you need to stop. Do only what your body can handle without hurting your muscles.

STRETCHING EXERCISES

Stretching is super for blood circulation and for good muscle condition. It helps to prevent muscle injuries during all sports and physical activities. After working each individual muscle area, you need to stretch the muscle in order to prevent muscle cramps or severe soreness. In addition, stretching makes muscles lean and smooth. In order to prevent a bulky look, integrate stretching into your exercise program. (If I have a busy schedule, I still stretch daily—it takes five to ten minutes.)

The stretching exercises are designated by a star (★) in the exercise program. You can skip the other exercises and do only the stretching exercises if your time is limited or if you have participated in a vigorous sport. As you grow stronger, double each set in this exercise program.

EXERCISE PROGRAM
(20 TO 30 MINUTES)

This program is designed so that you move from one exercise to the next without stopping.

WARM UP

Stretch your arms straight above your head. Keep your feet about 18 inches apart. Bend your right knee while reaching up with your right arm. Repeat on the left side. Come back to the beginning position. Bring your arms to shoulder level.

5 times each position

ARM MUSCLES

Keeping your arms in a straight line with your shoulders, stretch your arms out. Palms up. Rotate in circles clockwise 10 times. Rotate counterclockwise 10 times. Relax your arms to your sides.

20 forward, 20 back

★ SPINE STRETCH

Bring your arms to your back, lower your chest slowly by bending at the waist, keeping your chin up and your back flat. While your chest is waist level, press it gently toward the floor several times. Then slowly drop your chest and head toward your feet, dropping your arms to your toes at the same time. Press down gently.

5 times

76

THIGH WARM-UP

While standing bent over, press your toes down slowly, bend your right knee, then your left. Straighten your legs. Walk your feet out wider than your hips. Bring bent upper torso over your right thigh and bend your left knee. Hold. Straighten and come to center position. Repeat on the left side. Straighten to center position. Walk your hands out and slowly lower your knees to the floor.

5 times each position

PUSHUPS (ARM MUSCLES)

While on your knees with your arms straight under your shoulders (feet by your seat) bend your elbows and then straighten your arms. Repeat several times. Then push your seat back toward your feet and sit off to one side. Sit up in a relaxed position.

5 times

★ ARMS STRETCH

Reach your arms up, clasp your fingers, then turn your palms toward the ceiling. Push your arms back. Bend your elbows, taking your arms behind your head to the left. Push your head against your right elbow and hold. Repeat on the other side.

5 times each position

77

ABDOMEN MUSCLES

Bend your knees in a sitting position. Hold on to the back of each thigh, round your back (chin to chest), and push your spine back toward the floor. Release your arms. Using your stomach, lift your chest slowly to your knees, then push back to where the small of your back touches the floor. Repeat several times. On your last repetition, put your hands on the front of your thighs and slowly bring your hands and your upper torso down to the floor. Using your stomach muscles to slightly lift your torso, slide your hands to your knees, then back. Relax. Repeat. Lie down with your arms overhead, your legs out straight.

10 complete cycles

★ ABDOMEN STRETCH

Lying flat on the floor with your arms extended straight out over your head, arch your back slightly. Stretch up with your arms and stretch down with your feet. Relax, letting your back touch the floor. Repeat arch and stretch.

5 times

HIP/THIGH MUSCLES

Roll over to your left side. Bend your knees so that they are perpendicular to your chest and body. Lean on your elbow or your hand. Lift your entire right leg at one time. Don't let it flop and don't lead with your knee. Keeping position, push your leg to the back and lift in the same fashion. Straighten your leg and lift up several times. Repeat on the other side. Bend your knees and roll to your back.

20 times each position

78

★ HIP/THIGH STRETCH

While on your back, place your right ankle on your left knee. Keeping your left knee slightly bent, place your hands behind your thigh, bringing your knee close to your chest. Hold. Repeat with your other leg.

5 times

INNER THIGHS

Roll over to your left side, lean on your elbow, bend your right leg in front of your body. Extend your left leg out to your side or on the diagonal (whichever feels best to you) and lift your left leg several times. Repeat on the other side.

20 times each

★ WAIST AND THIGH STRETCH

Sitting up, spread your legs wide apart. Reach your right arm above your head. Drop your torso slowly to the left side. Stretch. Roll your chest over your leg, reach your right arm to your left toe. Stretch. Relax your arm, walk your hands to center. Press your chest down gently to the lowest point. (Don't force yourself.) Repeat on the other side.

5 times each position

79

BACK THIGH MUSCLES

Roll to your knees and hands. Arch your back. Extend your right leg straight back and lift while your stomach is very tight. Your hips stay level. Bend your knee and push your toes to the ceiling several times. Repeat on the other side. Come back to sitting position.

20 times each

COOL DOWN

Come back to your hands and knees, raise your hips and legs to a crawl position, crawl hands to toes. Stretch. Spread your legs wide, toes pointed out. Turn to the left side, press your chest to your left leg. Next point your toes up and press. Repeat on the other side. Move to the center.

10 times each

Stand up and feel great! Becoming the Best me is good for the inner and outer self, and achieving the Best Me shape is good for both too!

Materials

- ♥ "upbeat" music to exercise by
- ♥ cute exercise outfit
- ♥ exercise shoes

Tools

- ♥ jump rope

the best me
becoming a woman

♥ You're becoming a woman now, but becoming a full-grown, independent woman takes time. Your body must go through gradual, wonderful changes. So do your mind and your spirit. At times, the changes are exciting . . . other times bewildering.

Adolescence is the period of life when puberty begins (in girls, puberty usually occurs between the ages of nine and sixteen). During this time you experience many changes of growth and development. You can see outward changes. You grow taller, your body rounds out and looks more feminine, your breasts develop, your reproductive organs begin to function, and menstruation begins. Of all the many changes you are now experiencing, menstruation is perhaps the biggest mystery, but it doesn't have to be. Let's talk about it.

The purpose of menstruation is to prepare your body for the normal biological function of women—the ability to reproduce (to have children). Month after month, the menstrual cycle is repeated during the reproductive years of a woman's life. The average menstrual cycle is about twenty-eight days. A cycle is counted from the first day of menstruation until the first day of the next menstrual period. It can vary from twenty to thirty-five days and still be normal. Your cycle may be irregular for the first year or so, but after this time it should become regular. The length of each period varies. Some girls menstruate for only three days, some for as long as seven. However, the average menstrual period is about four or five days.

It's a good idea to keep a record of your menstrual cycle. (Your calendar/organizer will be useful for this.) Circle the days you menstruate. Start with the date you begin and end with the last day of your period. Do this each time you menstruate. After several menstrual periods, you will see a pattern. You will then know how long each of your cycles will be—how long your menstrual period lasts—and when it will come again.

QUESTIONS GIRLS OFTEN ASK

What do I do if I start menstruating for the first time while I'm at school?

A. You will want to be prepared for your period, no matter when it occurs. If you know about menstruation before it happens for the first time, you will be able to handle this situation without fear or embarrassment. If it does come unexpectedly, don't panic. At school, your teachers and school nurse know all about what is happening and usually can provide you with "emergency" menstrual protection. Once you begin to menstruate regularly, you will know when to expect your next period, and you can be prepared for it.

Can anyone tell by looking at me that I have my period?

A. No, unless your attitude and lack of good grooming indicate this. Very often girls worry about telltale signs. Fortunately, there really aren't any outward physical signs of the menstrual period. The important thing is to be especially careful about grooming and personal cleanliness.

Is it safe to bathe and wash my hair while menstruating?

A. Contrary to many beliefs and fears, it is perfectly safe. In fact, it is important to bathe because you perspire more during the menstrual period. Washing your hair won't stop the flow either. By keeping fresh and clean, you'll feel better.

Why do some girls have menstrual cramps?

A. Good menstrual health is closely related to general good health. Worrying about menstruation can do much toward tensing muscles and causing cramps. Mild cramps are sometimes made worse by poor health habits rather than menstruation itself. Constipation is also a contributing factor. Others are poor posture and, believe it or not, not enough exercise. Severe cramps, however, should be brought to the attention of a doctor.

What can I do to prevent menstrual discomfort?

A. There's a great deal you can do. Eat a well-balanced diet because good nutrition is important. To help prevent constipation, drink plenty of water and eat fresh fruits and vegetables. Stand and sit erect. Get enough sleep. Be sure you exercise because it increases circulation and helps to relieve tension that may cause cramping.

What kind of exercise?

A. All forms of exercise and sports activities are good, but I've included instructions for two special exercises recommended by a doctor. Try them for better posture and good muscle tone. You'll look and feel better—and they'll do wonders in preventing menstrual discomfort.

Do these exercises twice a day. They take just a few minutes and are easy to do.

Exercise 1:
1. Stand with your arms raised to shoulder level.
2. With your knees kept straight, twist your trunk toward the left, and bend till your right hand touches your left foot. Repeat four times with right hand, then four times with left hand to right foot.

Exercise 2:
1. Stand with your arms at your sides, feet parallel and a few inches apart.
2. Swing your arms forward and upward while raising your left leg vigorously backward. Repeat four times with left leg, four times with right.

Is what I eat important?

A. Nutrition is necessary for growth and general good health. Be sure you eat three well-balanced meals a day. Stay away from too many sweets, junk foods, carbonated drinks, and fried foods.

Your daily diet should include meat or fish, fruits, vegetables, dairy products, grains, and cereals to give you the proper nutrition you need. Proper diet will reduce the likelihood of constipation, and regular elimination is important to your general well being.

Practicing good health habits, eating properly, and being neat and well groomed will help you look and feel your best every day. If you are overly concerned about your period, this may be obvious to others. Your naturalness and poise will work together to prevent embarrassment. Eventually you learn to accept menstruation as a natural, normal part of your life.

How can I look and feel good when I'm menstruating?

A. Sometimes you have the blues right before your period. But they don't always have to come. Some girls expect them and almost make a habit of them. A smart girl won't give in to them. You can take your mind off yourself by doing things you enjoy such as dancing, reading, or listening to records. You'll find that being active helps you feel good and look happy too.

Notes

- ♥ eat properly
- ♥ try to get plenty of exercise & sleep
- ♥ work at keeping my attitude positive
- ♥ go about my life as usual!

CHAPTER NINE

the best me
body language

♥ Let's play a game. Stand up and, without saying anything, act out each of the following words:

1. *self-consciousness*
2. *self-confidence*
3. *anger*
4. *happiness*

5. *snobbishness*
6. *friendliness*
7. *wallflower*
8. *fashion model*

Analyze what you did each time to act out the word. Do you see any particular pattern in what you did? Did you make similar body movements for the odd numbered words and similar ones for the even numbered ones? Did you stand up straight with your head held high and have pleasing facial expressions for the even numbers, while you bent over, head down, and had unpleasant facial expressions for the odd numbers?

YOUR BODY SPEAKS

You speak as clearly to others through your body movements as you do with your words. In fact, you speak to them even more through your body, because your body is sending messages all the time, whether or not you are talking. When movies were first invented, they did not have any sound; consequently, the actors and actresses had to convey the story's message through body language and dress. Turn on the TV and turn down the sound. Study the characters and see what you can learn about them.

Years ago when I began my modeling career, I was tremendously impressed by the good posture and gracefulness of another model. She was not a beautiful person. Feature by feature, she was rather unattractive, but she had created an aura of beauty about herself simply by the way she carried herself. She held herself so high and moved so gracefully, you were convinced that she was a rare creature of extraordinary beauty. Whether or not you want to become a model, your posture and carriage can help you look like one. It is not an unchangeable or impossible dream. You can make another dream come true!

The next time you go to a fashion show, study the model's posture and grace. They would not be on the runway unless they had learned how to carry themselves correctly. Correct posture is the key to moving gracefully whether you are walking, going up and down steps, sitting, or getting in and out of a car.

Poor posture can make the most beautiful outfit seem less than ordinary. It can cause the hemline to look uneven and wrinkles and lines to appear in the outfit. This is another reason a model's posture is so important. Clothes are to hang on the body without any of the lines being distorted. Have you ever heard someone say about another person, "She could put on anything and look good"? Girls who wear clothes well have two things in common: a trim, well-proportioned figure and good carriage. You can have both too.

YOUR POSTURE AFFECTS YOU PHYSICALLY

In addition to giving others a message, your posture also affects you physically. Poor posture can cause curvature of the spine, backache, and back strain. When your chest is slumped forward, your lungs are affected, causing your oxygen supply to be lowered. Your insides, such as the female organs, diaphragm, liver, and stomach, may fall or sag too. Even leg muscle strain can result from the body's being unbalanced. You cannot feel or look your best with these problems.

TAKE A POSTURE TEST

From a side view of yourself in a full-length mirror, check these points:

Head	☐	erect	☐	down
	☒	normal	☐	forward
Shoulders	☐	straight	☒	rounded
Back	☒	straight	☐	curved
			☐	swayback
Derriere (bottom)	☒	tucked under	☐	protruding
Tummy	☒	flat	☐	bulging
Knees	☒	slightly flexed	☐	locked

89

POSTURE IMPROVERS

Does your posture need a little help? Try one or more of the following exercises.

1. Lie on the floor with your bottom touching the baseboard and your legs straight up the wall (your legs will be at right angles to your body). This is excellent for lower back pain too.

   5 minutes per day

2. Lie on the floor with your arms stretched straight back over your head. Bend your knees and keep your feet flat on the floor. Pull in your tummy and press the small of your back to the floor. Hold a few seconds, then relax.

   10 times per day

3. Sit with your legs crossed Indian style and your back against a wall. With your arms bent at right angles at the elbow and hands pointed toward the ceiling, place your arms flat against the wall with elbows at shoulder level. Keeping head, shoulders, elbows, and wrists against the wall, slide your arms up as far as you can without losing contact with the wall. Slowly slide arms down. Repeat.

   10 times per day

4. You can take a beauty break and help your posture too when you lie on a slant board. You can purchase one or use your mom's ironing board. Elevate one end twelve to fifteen inches high. Place your head at the low end and your feet at the high end. By reversing the pull of gravity, you will receive many benefits. Your complexion and scalp

will tingle from the increased blood circulation. Your muscles will relax from the reversal of the downward pull on them. Reversing the pull of gravity is great for your feet and legs because it allows accumulated congestion to be released in the blood stream. And it's super for your posture—your spine straightens out, and your back flattens itself. You will feel like a new person.

15 minutes, twice a day

During my busy modeling days, I would come home after standing on my feet all day and stretch out for about twenty minutes on my slant board. I would feel more relaxed than if I had taken an hour's nap.

For many years the great beauties have used a slant board. Try it, you'll like it! Get into the habit now while you are in your teens.

POSTURE PERFECT

I want to teach you, step by step, how to stand with your body in correct posture. Before we begin, stand as you normally do. Observe yourself. You probably have all of your weight on one leg with your hip thrown to one side. Feel around your waist. Your upper body has settled into your waist, and if you have any excess pounds, you will be able to feel a roll or two. Standing correctly can give you the illusion of losing five to ten pounds of body weight.

Now to begin. Preferably wearing leotards and body suit, you should stand in front of a full-length mirror. Place your feet side by side a few inches apart with your toes pointing straight ahead. Your weight should be equally distributed between both feet. Your weight should be on the entire area of each foot, not to the inside or outside of the foot, or to the front or back. You want to have a solid foundation.

Next, relax your knees, but not so much that they are bent. When you are nervous, you have a tendency to lock your knees and hold your fists tight. You can cause yourself to pass out from standing in such a tense way because your blood flow and oxygen supply are restricted. Loosen up!

Become familiar with your "elevator muscles." They are in your thighs. If you are not quite sure where they are, do this little exercise. Pretend a pencil is lying parallel to your right foot. With your back perfectly straight and your chin parallel to the floor, go straight down and pick up the pencil. When we do this exercise in "The Teen I Want to Be" Workshops, I can hear a chorus of snaps, crackles and pops—and yes, everyone feels those elevator muscles.

Instead of using the elevator muscles for lifting, walking, sitting, and going up and down stairs, most people use their backs. By learning to use your elevator muscles, you'll prevent serious back problems caused by putting too much stress on your back.

Let's move to the derriere (bottom). Tilt your pelvis forward and up. If this sounds too complicated, just imagine a dog tucking its tail. You tuck your bottom under in the same way. (Remember to pull in your tummy too.) The pelvic bones are very important to good posture. If they are tilted down, you will have a swayback and a protruding tummy. To work on holding your pelvic bones correctly, do the following exercise, called the "Pelvic Rock," several times a day.

Standing in correct posture, put one hand on your tummy and one on your bottom. Rock your pelvic area forward and up. Now relax! See how your hips tuck under? Repeat this several times. You may feel like you're doing a belly dance but go ahead, the exercise is great for you!

Have you ever been told to hold your shoulders back? Well, I have good news for you. Relax and let them go! Shake all the tension out.

Raise each shoulder toward the ear. Now rotate them backward. Rotate them forward. Relax again. Is all of the tension gone? When you hold your chest correctly, your shoulders fall into proper place.

Imagine that you have a wishbone between your breasts with a string attached to it. Now imagine the string is being pulled up, up, up . . . straight up toward the ceiling. Feel how elongated your torso becomes as you lift your chest up with the pull of the string. Your waist is now trimmed down and pulled out of your hips. You have lots of room to breathe and your shoulders are hanging naturally in place.

Attach an imaginary string to the top of your head. Pull your head up so that it pulls your neck back and out of your shoulders. Pull until your chin is parallel to the floor.

Look in the mirror. Smile. You are posture perfect. Get the feel clearly imprinted in your mind and in your muscles. Practice until this way of standing becomes a habit.

HOW A MODEL STANDS

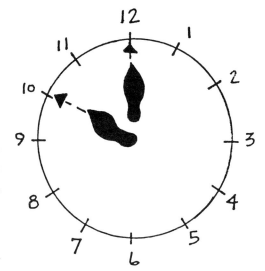

BASIC STANCE

- Draw an imaginary clock on the floor.
- Place your right foot at twelve o'clock.
- Place your left foot at ten o'clock, fitting the instep of the left foot to the heel of the right foot. Leaving the left foot pointed at the same angle, pull it back several inches (no more than six inches) until you feel comfortable and stable.
- Shift your weight to your left foot.
- Slightly relax your right knee.
- Position your legs so there is no space showing between them at any

93

point. Check the mirror for the position that makes your legs look the most attractive.

• Turn your body toward ten o'clock.
• Keep your chin parallel to the floor and point directly to twelve o'clock.

Try reversing the process with your left foot forward.

You are now standing like a model, and there are some good reasons for standing this way. First of all, it is flattering to your legs. When you stand with your legs side by side and have space between them, any feature of your legs that is less than perfect becomes obvious.

WHAT ARE THE "GIVENS" IN YOUR LEGS?

Normal ☐
Thin ☐
Bowed ☐
Heavy ☐
Knock-kneed ☐

Whatever the givens, you can create an illusion to make your legs appear normal by learning how to stand in the basic model's stance.

This posture can also make your figure appear thinner and shapelier, which is especially important if you are on television or do photography modeling because the camera makes you appear ten pounds heavier. Who can afford that? By positioning yourself at an angle, you shift the center focal point of your body. You have fooled the eye because now only one-half of your body is fully seen. (The body also shows lovelier curves.)

Another helpful thing to know about the basic model's stance is that if you ever have to stand in one place for a long time, this position gives you three ways to distribute your body weight without anyone knowing that you have moved. You can alternate the three ways and then start over. You start out with (1) your weight on your back foot, (2) then shift to your front foot, and (3) then distribute your weight between both feet. A lifesaver, especially if you ever do "freeze" modeling!

MODEL'S PIVOT

A pivot is used in modeling to turn in order to show the front and back of an outfit you are wearing and to change direction on the runway. It is used the same way in beauty pageants.

Half-Pivot

Standing in your basic position, shift your weight to the ball of your front foot. Slightly raise your heels off the floor and make a half-turn in the direction that your back foot is pointing. If you start out with your right foot pointing toward twelve and your left foot pointing toward ten, turn counterclockwise toward the ten. Now your left foot should be pointing toward six and your right foot toward eight. Turn back again to the original position. Practice turning back and forth without moving from the same spot. Change foot positions. Start with your left foot forward. Practice. Practice. Practice.

Let's add a step to the pivot. Get in your basic position, weight on your back foot (left). Step forward first with your front foot (right), then move left foot forward and ahead of right foot making a straight line. Then repeat with your right foot. Then stop and turn slowly. Pause and get yourself back into your basic position. Repeat left, right, left, turn. Do this over and over until your pivots are smooth and graceful.

Complete Pivot

A complete pivot is a little more complicated to do, but it's a lot of fun and looks great on the runway, especially if you are wearing something with movement and fullness. As you are walking, place your right foot around to the outside of your left foot (you have crossed your leg over). With both heels off the floor and your weight on the balls of your feet, turn to the left until you are completely around and in the same direction you started. Continue walking. When you have learned to do the turn gracefully to the left, practice placing your left foot around your right and turning to the right.

A complete pivot is good to use just before you exit the runway, so that you are turning once more to the audience as a sort of final contact. Never just walk down the runway and off with your back to the audience the entire time. That is too impersonal.

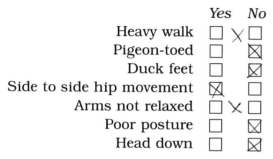

	Yes	No
Heavy walk	✕	
Pigeon-toed		☒
Duck feet		☒
Side to side hip movement	☒	
Arms not relaxed	✕	
Poor posture		☒
Head down		☒

THE GRACEFUL WALK

Has your mother ever told you that you sound like a horse walking through the house? Do you have a heavy walk? Do you clomp, clomp along? If so, you are probably putting your heels down very hard at the beginning of each step. Oh, you don't know how you walk? Get a friend to watch you and give you some feedback.

If the answer was yes to any of these characteristics, you need some help. Get a piece of chalk and a yard stick. Draw a straight line on the floor or carpet (it will brush off). Work in front of a full-length mirror if you can. Try to allow enough space in front of the mirror for your basic stance, five steps, and a pivot.

Practice with dressy shoes on, preferably closed-toe pumps, with a medium height heel, not with tennis shoes or backless shoes. Shoes affect the way you walk and pivot. In tennis shoes, you have a tendency to walk in a more boyish manner, and the rubber soles will not allow you to pivot easily. When you wear backless shoes, you are constantly using your toes to try to keep your shoes on your feet.

Starting at the end of the line farthest from the mirror, get into your basic stance with your right foot pointed toward twelve and your left foot pointed toward ten. Make sure you are standing correctly with knees slightly flexed, hips tucked under, chest up, and chin parallel to the floor. Shift your weight to your left foot. Step out with your right foot, about the length of one of your own feet, and step down, placing the inside ball of your right foot on the line. Now bring your left foot about one foot length ahead of your right foot and place down with the inside ball of your left foot touching the line and the heel on the line. (This procedure keeps you from looking as if you are walking a tight-rope.)

The legs move out from the waist with a forward movement rather than a side to side movement. Be sure to keep your head and eyes up and your chin parallel to the floor so that you are showing your pretty face (wear a big smile too!). The movement is mostly in the lower body. Try to move on a straight plane without bobbing up and down. To accomplish this, try the old trick of walking with a book on your head.

Repeat the steps until you have taken five. Pivot on the fifth step. Return to starting position. Practice every day until you don't need the chalk line as a guide.

A REVIEW OF THE GRACEFUL WALK

1. Stand correctly.
2. Steps should be about the length of one of your feet (from toe of back foot to heel of forward foot).
3. Toes point straight ahead or ever so slightly out with heels on a straight line.
4. Knees slightly flexed.
5. Hips move forward from the waist, not side to side.
6. Keep weight evenly on the balls of your feet, and use the ball of your back foot to push forward.
7. Your arms swing in the opposite direction from your feet for balance.

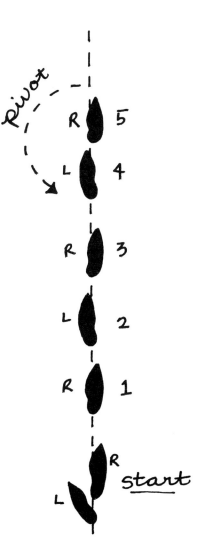

8. Let your arms be relaxed and swing naturally from the shoulders.
9. Don't bob up and down. Your head should move on a straight plane. The movement is in the lower body.
10. Imagine you are walking on eggshells!

SUGGESTIONS FOR SPECIFIC PROBLEMS

Heavy walk. Practice walking on the chalk line, putting your toes down first on the line in a pointed, exaggerated way. Imagine that you are gliding on ice. Feels silly, doesn't it? If you practice this enough, you will lighten your walk and avoid putting your weight down heel first. (Don't practice this going down the hall at school.)

Pigeon-toed. Practice walking on the chalk line, with heels on the line and toes pointed slightly outward.

Duck feet. Practice walking on the line with toes and heels always exactly on the line.

Head down. Just for fun, practice walking with a book on your head. You will have to keep your chin parallel to the floor and avoid bobbing up and down so much.

GOING UP AND DOWN STAIRS

When going up and down stairs, keep your body in correct posture with your back straight, using your elevator muscles in your legs. Place your foot at a slight angle and well onto the step. Keep your knees flexed and close together. Hold your head up and look down with your eyes if you need to.

When going up and down stairs in an evening gown, lift the gown at the points where your hands fall. Don't bend down to pick it up. Gently lift it enough to clear your steps, then let it gracefully fall back down. You will look like a queen!

SITTING GRACEFULLY

Let's now combine what you've learned about walking with some pointers on sitting. Place a chair at the end of the chalk line with the chair back to the mirror (so you can see yourself approach the chair).

1. Walk to the chair and pivot. Try to gauge it so that when you pivot, your back leg is slightly touching the front of the chair seat. If you pivoted too soon, take a step backward until you feel the chair. Don't lean over, stick your bottom out, and turn to see if the chair is there.

2. The secret to sitting down is to keep your back perfectly straight. Using your elevator muscles in your thighs, lower your body straight down to the front edge of the chair. Your hips remain tucked under. Again, avoid leading with your bottom.

3. Using both hands on the edge of the chair and keeping your back straight, slide smoothly back. Don't wiggle your hips backward. If you are short or have short legs, it is not necessary to slide all the way to the back of the chair and leave your feet dangling.

4. You may smooth your skirt under you with your hands when you are in the process of sitting.

5. Sit at a slight angle with your knees together and either to the right or left with your feet remaining in the basic position.

6. Keep your hands relaxed and placed to one side.

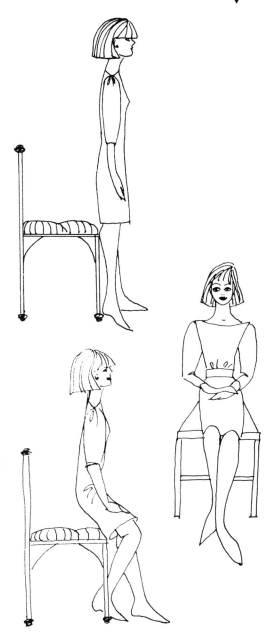

99

OTHER SITTING POSITIONS

Feet crossed at the ankles. With your feet in the basic position, bring your back foot back and around your forward foot. Your feet are crossed at the ankle.

Legs crossed above the knees. Crossing your legs at the knees cuts off circulation and causes many health problems, such as varicose veins. It is also unattractive. Furthermore, because the upper leg is extended too far out, the possibility of tripping someone exists! If you must cross your legs (if you are long legged like I am, you probably will), cross them well above the knees at the thigh area. Keep your legs close together with the toes of your upper leg close to the ankle of your lower leg. Shift both legs and feet slightly to the right if your lower leg is the right leg; to the left if your lower leg is the left leg. Place your hands one on top of the other on your upper thigh in a relaxed manner.

ARISING FROM A CHAIR

It is easier to sit down in a chair than to get up because gravity helps you down but it works against you in getting up. To arise gracefully:

1. Place your feet in the basic position.

2. Using both hands, with your back kept straight during the entire process, slide to the front edge of the chair.

3. Use your back foot to push with and your elevator muscles to lift yourself to a standing position. You are in the basic foot position and ready to walk off.

GETTING IN AND OUT OF A CAR

Getting in and out of a car is one of the most difficult things to learn to do gracefully—and with some cars it is next to impossible! A special challenge is getting into the back seat of a two-door car without looking clumsy or hanging yourself on the seat belts. Oh, well, here goes. At least you can try for improvement.

Entering, Standard Four-Door Car

1. After the door is opened, stand facing the front of the car (your left side to the right side of the car or vice versa) with your leg almost touching the car. Your feet should be close together.
2. Place your left foot inside the car.
3. Turn slightly and slide into the seat.
4. Bring the other foot into the car.

Another correct way is to stand facing the front of the car, turn slightly and sit, then bring both feet into the car.

Exiting, Standard Four-Door Car

1. Slide over to the door.
2. Put your right foot out and onto the ground.
3. Lift your body with your left foot which is inside the car and get out.

Or you may prefer to swing your body around and place both feet on the ground. Use your left hand to push yourself out.

Entering Back Seat, Two-Door Car

1. Using your elevator muscles, stoop and step in.
2. Bring other foot in, turn and sit.
   Good luck! Hope you didn't get strangled on the seat belt.

Exiting Back Seat, Two-Door Car

1. Slide as close to the door as possible.
2. Extend your head and one leg, then bring out your other leg. Don't get out bottom first!

COATS AND ACCESSORIES

Have you ever wished that you could be as graceful as a model is when she takes off her coat on the runway? Or perhaps look the way she looks carrying her handbag or umbrella? What style! What class! This is certainly a possible dream. You can master it too!

COATS

Get your coat and stand in front of your full-length mirror.

1. Hold your coat in the middle of the back neckline with the lining facing you.
2. Put your right arm into the sleeve and slide the coat well up onto your right shoulder.
3. Grasp the right lapel with your right hand.
4. Reach in back with your left hand and find the left sleeve and put your arm into it.
5. Adjust your coat with both hands on the lapels.
6. Button the coat from the top down.

Taking your coat off looks a lot more glamorous and is more fun than putting it on. Don't you love to see a model on a runway remove her coat? You can learn how to do it exactly the same way she does.

1. Grasp your coat at the lapels and push it back off your shoulders.
2. With your hands behind your back, grasp the left sleeve and with your right hand and take your left arm out of the sleeve.

102

3. Bring the sleeve ends to the front and take them with your left hand.

4. Remove your right arm from the sleeve.

5. Grasp the middle back of the coat at the neck and let it hang into a neat fold.

6. Carry folded on your left arm or hang the coat up. Another way to carry it, if you are on the runway, is to grasp it at the center back neck and carry it over one shoulder. The lining of the coat is *never* turned to the outside.

ACCESSORIES

The key to all of your accessories is to keep them under control and close to your body. No loose, flying objects, please! Watch those pocketbooks and umbrellas if you don't want to look like Mary Poppins flying through the air.

Shoulder bag. Place the strap on your left shoulder if you are right-handed. This will leave your right hand free. Place the bag parallel to your line of walk. Hold it close by grasping the top front corner with your left hand, your thumb to the inside.

Envelopes. You can carry an envelope or clutch bag several different ways. You can tuck it under your arm. You can carry it in your left hand with your index finger along the bottom of the bag toward the front corner. Or you may carry it with your finger in the same position but on the top of the bag.

Handle bag. Carry a bag with a handle at arm's length, parallel to your line of walk.

Tote bag. A tote bag is carried the same way as a bag with a handle. If the handle is long enough, you can put it on your shoulder and carry it as a shoulder bag.

PRACTICE, PRACTICE, PRACTICE

All of the exercises in this chapter take practice. You may feel awkward at first, but keep at it. Soon it will be second nature to you just as it is to the models you admire. Regardless of your givens, you can create an aura of beauty about yourself by the way you carry your body. Stand up tall and straight, whether you are five feet tall or six feet tall, with pride and dignity, and be counted!

Notes

♥ improve my posture
♥ practice basic model stance, pivot & walk

Tools

♥ full-length mirror

practice!!

CHAPTER TEN

how to
become a model

WOULD YOU LIKE TO BE A MODEL?

♥ Do you want to become a model someday? Girls dream of becoming models probably more often than they dream about other career choices. I was no different. As a child and a teen-ager I dreamed that too. It proved to be a possible dream for me, and for many years I enjoyed an exciting career as a fashion and photography model.

Do you dream of an agent discovering you and making you a top model overnight? Sorry, it rarely happens that way. Becoming a successful model is much like becoming successful in any other profession. You must have the right physical requirements, a burning desire, common sense, knowledge, ability, and persistence. Remember, there is a price to be paid for anything worthwhile, and being a model is hard work.

I get calls almost daily from teen-agers (or their mothers calling for them) asking for advice on how to get into the modeling field. I like to ask these girls some questions and give them some facts in order to help them make realistic decisions. If they think it through and they still want to pursue modeling careers, I help them develop strategies to reach that goal.

Let's pretend we are sitting together in my office, sipping a cool soft drink and talking about your desire to become a model. I would start out by asking you: "Why do you want to be a model?" Write down your answer just as though you were talking to me.

• I want to become a model because . . .

_____

_____

Do you think the career would make you a more desirable and worthwhile person? Do you think modeling would be fun? Do you want to be famous and see yourself in magazines? Do you love fashion and design? Do you want to express your creativity? Have you heard models make a lot of money? Be as specific as you can. Sometimes after thinking something through very carefully, you realize that your reasons are not solid enough to give you the commitment to reach your goal.

What about school? Do you plan to finish high school, or do you plan to pursue your modeling career full-time now? Do you plan to go to college? I encourage every girl I counsel to get her education. Make your education your top priority. Majoring in fashion will not help you become a model. Major in music, education, science, fashion merchandising, or whatever you have an interest in and a bent toward. After graduation, you can then make the decision about the field you want to go into full-time.

Very few models have a long career of modeling. In the major fashion centers of the world, a qualified model has the opportunity for a lot of work, but she usually has a short life span of modeling. In smaller cities, less work is available, but the model's career is longer. For instance, I modeled much longer in Atlanta, the fashion center of the South, than I could have in New York, the major fashion center of the United States and one of the top four centers in the world. A city smaller than Atlanta probably would have provided an even longer life span of modeling but less work. Like most models, I chose to leave the modeling field before it chose to leave me. After eighteen years of a rewarding career, I began a new business, Mary Ann Green & Associates, an image-consulting firm. "The Teen I Want To Be" Workshops, taught nationwide, are a part of this business. You too need other career possibilities in your life. That is why it's so important to get an education.

PHYSICAL REQUIREMENTS

Next you need to consider your physical assets. How tall are you? _____ feet _____ inches (measure height without shoes). How much do you weigh? _____ pounds.

Ideally, a model is five seven to five nine. (High-fashion models can be taller than five nine). You will be very limited in fashion modeling if you are less than five six. Fashion modeling requires a person who can fit easily into ready-made, standard-length clothes without alterations. Junior and petite modeling may be the only available fashion work for you. Height is not as crucial for photography and commercial modeling, so if you are shorter or taller than the specified heights, you may want to investigate these areas.

Many models weigh up to five pounds less than the weight for the smallest frame for their height shown on the Weight Chart (see Chapter 6). There are a number of reasons for this. The garment is to hang on

BE WISE

There are many good, reputable agencies, but there are also many unscrupulous people in the business. It is very important that your parents be involved in your pursuing a model agency to represent you. You and your parents will want to be on the lookout for warning signals. Be very wise in relation to the way an agent advertises.

the body from the shoulder line and not be distorted in any way. This requires a slim body! In addition, a camera creates an illusion that makes the person look five to ten pounds heavier. The model must compensate for this illusion by weighing less. Last, sorry to say, we live in a society that thinks thin is beautiful.

Before you get discouraged and jump to the conclusion that you are not model material, let me quickly say you do not have to be perfect or beautiful to be a model. Some of the most famous models have less than perfect features. They do not all have an "ideal" oval-shaped face, flawless features, and perfectly proportioned bodies. In fact, some super models did not feel very pretty as children and, as a result, developed a great drive to create their own style and aura of beauty. Many times the "ugly duckling" turned "beautiful swan" has the most charisma to project to the audience. That is not to say that if you are naturally beautiful you have a strike against you. (Beauty pageants are often an entree into the modeling world.) The only time being beautiful is a disadvantage is when you have not developed your inner qualities and have sailed through life on your looks alone.

A MODEL IS AN ACTRESS

In addition to the right physical requirements, a model needs to be able to move to music well. She becomes an actress as she projects to the audience or to the camera the mood the designer intended for the design to create. The mood changes with each outfit and each designer.

GETTING STARTED

We have talked about the requirements for modeling. Now let's talk about how you get started. First of all, you have to take into consideration the city in which you plan to model. New York, London, Paris, and Milan are the fashion centers of the world. Los Angeles and Chicago offer a lot of fashion work also. Atlanta and Dallas have the major apparel marts in the southern part of the United States, but only a few models can make modeling a full-time profession in these cities. How much fashion work is available in your city? A realistic assessment and knowledge of the fashion aspects of the city in which you intend to work are crucial. Modeling is more than just a fabulous dream.

THE MODEL AGENCY

The more fashion work there is in a city, the more important a model agency becomes to you. Because the agency gives you exposure to a wide range of clients, books jobs for you, and collects your fees, it is invaluable to your modeling career. Find out all you can about the agencies, then get in touch with the best, most creditable ones.

Most agencies do not make appointments on the first contact but will ask you to send photographs of yourself and a resume before they consent to interview you. Instead of hiring a photographer to take a lot of expensive pictures, get a friend who is good with a camera to take some shots of you. Create as many different looks as you possibly can to show your versatility. Send the best shots along with your resume to the agency.

If the agency feels there is a possibility that you have the look its clients want, you will be asked to come in for an interview. If you are not accepted by the agency, ask for advice. Is there another agency in town that capitalizes on your look or your age range? Do you need to improve or change anything? Make the most of the interview, and learn all you can that will be to your advantage.

PROTECT YOURSELF

Public solicitation by a so-called agent in the want ad section is to be steered clear of. Ads in newspapers or trade journals for "new faces" with "no experience necessary" for modeling and commercials are danger signs. Many unscrupulous people advertise using a name that sounds similar to a legitimate agency. If an agent asks for a "registration fee," beware. Legitimate agents work strictly on a commission basis. The phony agent may also try to get you to have expensive photographs made or to take lessons from a particular person or school.

After interviewing with several agencies, you will be in a position to make a decision about which one (or ones) would serve your needs best if you have the opportunity to sign with them. Be very cautious. Don't get so excited about the possibility of modeling that you do not use good judgment. Wait and see how well an agency represents you before you sign an exclusive contract. Of course, you may get rejections from the agencies but do not take it personally. The modeling field is no place to be if you can't take being turned down. After having the right physical requirements, it's a matter of being in the right place at the right time. The same agency that rejects you today may pick you up two weeks later. Persistence is a necessary quality for a model.

After you sign with an agency, you will need to work with a photographer to make some test shots. Many good, reputable photographers will do test shots for the cost of the film. (Yes, take your mom with you.) From those shots, the agency will select a photograph to use for the headsheet. (The *headsheet* contains photographs and information about all the models the agency represents.) If you go to all the expense of having pictures made before you go to an agency, you will have to do it all over again. Don't do anything prematurely.

After your work has begun and you accumulate test shots and on-the-job photographs of yourself, you will need to have a composite made. (The *composite* is the model's large business card.) It should have two to ten photographs of yourself in a range of different looks, as well as your name, sizes, and agency. The agency keeps a supply of your composite to send to interested clients who have seen your picture on the headsheet, and you carry a supply as you make your rounds. In addition you will develop a portfolio to show to prospective clients. A portfolio is a collection of your best photographs carried in what looks like a giant, flat briefcase.

FREE-LANCE WORK

Many department stores and boutiques book their models directly through their fashion offices. When this is the case, you need to make an appointment for an interview with the fashion coordinator of each store. This type of work is called "free-lance work." You handle your own bookings and finances. Many models work through an agency and do free-lance work too. If you plan to free lance, be sure this is covered in any agency contracts or you may be unable to do any work other than that provided by the agency.

MODELING SCHOOLS

The question I am asked most often about modeling is, "Should I go to a modeling school?" No, it is not necessary. Be wary of any modeling school that promises to turn you into a professional model. It can't make you a star, but it can take a lot of your money! If you have the potential to be a model, you can do it with or without a modeling school. The agency or the fashion coordinators interested in you will train you or will direct you to the help you need. Often it is preferable to have no training so you don't have to unlearn something you have been taught. The best training is on-the-job experience.

Understand that I am not against modeling schools. I attended one and found it beneficial to me. Later I was director of finishing and modeling for two schools. My teachers also modeled professionally. They knew the current way of doing things and had a lot of good ideas and contacts. The school is only as good as its teachers, so be sure to find out the qualifications of the people teaching you. A national chain modeling school may be great in one part of the country and very poor in another. Ask to audit a class before enrolling. Beware of high pressure sales tactics, such as, "You must sign today to take advantage of this once-in-a-lifetime offer." Use the same good judgment about a school as you do about an agency.

If you and your parents have any qualms about a school or agency, check with the Better Business Bureau as well as the unions to which professional performers belong—AFTRA (American Federation of Television and Radio Artists), AEA (Actors Equity Association), SAG (Screen Actors Guild), and AGMA (American Guild of Musical Artists). Your city also may have a Models Guild. Have your mom or dad call the Attorney General's office in your state to see whether any lawsuits have been brought against the agency or school you are considering.

A long-term modeling course may not be for you, but do take advantage of any workshops or activities that will give you experience and confidence. Enroll in "The Teen I Want to Be" Workshops, volunteer to model in charity fashion shows, enter beauty pageants. When I was seventeen years old, I won a statewide beauty pageant, and years later I became Mrs. Atlanta. Jodi was Miss Westwood High School and was selected to be on the Rich's Teen Board before she began modeling professionally. These activities were all a part of giving us the confidence we needed to make it in the modeling world.

In addition to conducting "The Teen I Want to Be" Workshops, my staff and I work with girls on both a private and group basis to assess their modeling or pageant potential and work out a program specifically for them. My goal is to help the teen become a more confident, radiant, self-assured young woman—a winner in life—whether or not she becomes a beauty queen or a professional model!

JODI GREEN   RICH'S TEEN BOARD

112

Notes

♥ attend "The Teen I Want To Be" Workshop

♥ be on the look out for fashion shows + pageants I can be in

♥ get a friend to take some photographs of me

Become a model teen-ager regardless of whether or not you become a teen-ager who models!

the best me hair style

♥ Have you ever considered the amount of time you spend thinking about and caring for your hair? Hair may be a lot of trouble, but it certainly is important. When you look at someone, it is the first thing you see, and it says a lot about who that person is. Your facial features are unchangeable, but you can do many possible things with your hair!

HEALTHY HAIR

Healthy hair is the result of a healthy body and proper hair care. The cutest style can never make up for limp, dull, damaged hair. Make the health of your hair your first priority. Be sure you are getting all the nutrients your body needs by eating from the Basic Four food groups. Eliminate junk foods. Pay particular attention to your protein and B vitamins. Take a multi-vitamin supplement daily to ensure your needs are being met.

Crash dieting or consistently eating too few calories per day can cause your hair to fall out. An underfed body simply can't furnish the hair with the food it needs.

Furthermore, drugs, alcohol, and cigarettes are murder to the hair! They harm the body and rob it of essential nutrients, all of which directly affects the hair. Any chemical put into the body shows up in the hair strand.

Do not damage your hair by abusing it with the sun, saltwater, or wind.

FLATTERING HAIR STYLE

You need to know a number of things in order to find the most flattering hair style for yourself.

FACE SHAPES

Do you know the shape of your face? If you don't, here are some things you can do to find out: (1) First of all, ask a friend. It's fun to try to analyze each other's shape and get an objective opinion. (2) If you still aren't quite sure of the shape, get in front of a mirror, and with soap, lipstick, or washable paints, draw the outline of your face onto the mirror. What is the shape you have drawn? (3) The most accurate way to determine your face shape is to have someone take a picture of you, from shoulder level up, with your hair pulled back from your face. Place tracing paper on the photograph (a blown-up one would be great), and draw a vertical line down the center of your face. Next, draw horizontal lines across your face from temple to temple, across the widest part of your cheekbones, and across the widest part of your jaw (under lower lip). Compare your face with the drawing here.

Now study the following drawings to see which hair styles are the most flattering for each face shape.

115

My face shape is _oval shaped_.

My least attractive facial feature is ___Nose___.

My neck is average __X__ short _____ long _____.

My height is __5"5'__.

The texture of my hair is _____.

My hair is thin _____ thick __X__.

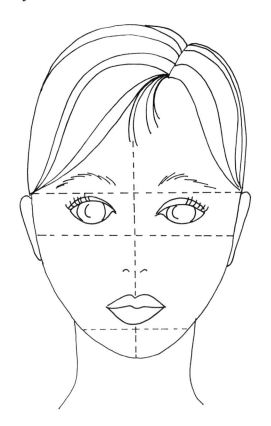

Face Shapes

*The Best Me
Hair Style*

Oval

The oval face is considered the ideal shape. You can wear almost any hair style.

Round

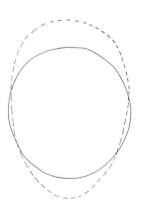

The round face has full cheeks and a round jawline. You are best with height on top, sides close to the face, and asymmetrical lines.

Heart

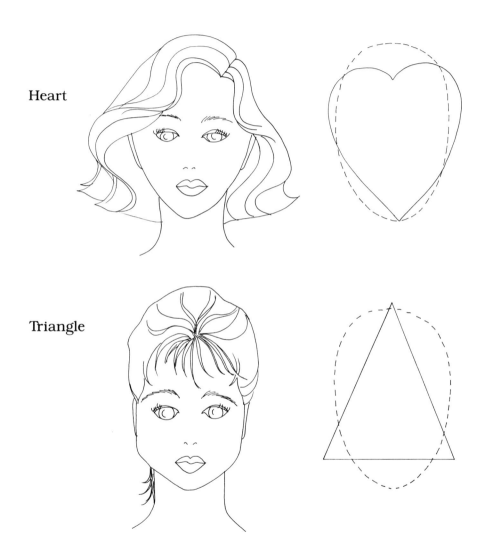

The heart-shaped face has a wide forehead and a narrow chin. You are best with width and fullness at the lower part of the face, a high part, and softness or side bangs.

Triangle

The triangle-shaped face has a narrow forehead and a wide chin. You are best with width at and above the temples. Avoid fullness at chin line.

117

Diamond

 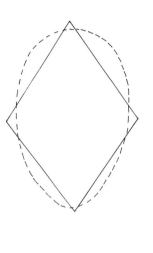

The diamond-shaped face has a narrow forehead and chin, with width across the cheekbones. You are best with hair close to the head at the cheekbone area with fullness above and below.

Square

 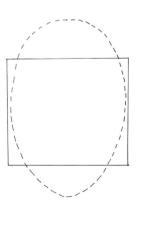

The square-shaped face has width across the forehead and chin. You are best with an asymmetrical hair style and height at the crown. Avoid bangs or width at the chin.

118

Oblong

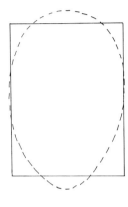

The oblong-shaped face is narrow with length. You are best with a soft, partial bang and fullness at sides. Avoid a center part and long straight hair.

THE ART OF GETTING THE MOST FROM A HAIR STYLIST

If trying to determine your face shape and best hair style is too complicated, just relax. There are professionals for that very purpose, but you need to know how to benefit from their services. Let's assume you have made the big decision to get help. Your goal is to find a fabulous new hair style that is just right for you. Here are some steps I suggest to help you achieve that goal:

1. *Make an appointment with a hair stylist you feel will be able to work best with your particular type of hair.* In order to find the right stylist, ask friends, whose hair styles you admire, for the names of their hair stylist. Don't hesitate to ask a stranger this question if she has a

THE TEEN I WANT TO BE

cut you really like. Save your money and go to the best (which incidentally is not always the most expensive).

2. *When you go for your appointment, wear clothes and make-up that project the image you want.* This will be very helpful to your hair stylist. If his or her first image of you is very trendy, you will have a hard time conveying your desire for a conservative hair style or vice versa.

3. *Before your hair is shampooed, talk with your hair stylist. Communication is the key.* Your hair stylist is not a mind reader. As I talk with hair stylists across the country, they make this point the most often. Over and over they tell me that teen-agers come in and either do not say anything about what they want or they are not clear. Then the teen-ager ends up in tears over the result. Believe me, this is difficult on hair stylists too, because their business depends on pleasing the customer. Be as specific as you can. Take pictures of styles you like. Be very clear about the length. Nothing is worse than having your hair cut three or four inches shorter than you had wanted. Also, be very honest in telling your stylist if you have had any chemical treatments on your hair such as perms, bleaching, coloring and, yes, even sun streaking. Tell about your lifestyle as well as the amount of time you spend on your hair daily. Now it's the stylist's turn. Listen carefully to what this professional tells you. The picture you have brought may not work for your hair. A modified version might do better. Remember to listen but do not be intimidated. Speak up! Ask questions. Ask about the cost. Feel comfortable with the style and cost before you begin. If the stylist is not willing to give you five to ten minutes before you begin, do not allow that person to do your hair!

4. *Have the stylist teach you how to take care of your hair.* You will want to know about such things as blowing your hair dry, using hot rollers and curling iron, and how often you need to have your hair cut.

Ask about recommended hair products for your type of hair . . . don't feel, though, that you have to buy them on the spot if the products are sold at the salon.

HOME MAINTENANCE "HOW TO'S"

SHAMPOOING TIPS

If you are like most teen-agers, you shampoo your hair every day. That may be necessary—or it may not. Try skipping the shampoo every other day for a while. If your hair is normal or dry, it will probably work to your advantage. Think about the time you have saved. If your hair is very oily, you will probably need to go back to shampooing every day. Shampoo the least often you can to maintain the shiny, bouncy look you want.

Here are some hints that can help you get the most out of your shampooing.

1. *Combine your shampoo with your morning shower.* You will save time and have the advantage of lots of water.

2. *Wet your hair thoroughly with lukewarm water as soon as you get into the shower.* While your hair is absorbing the water, cleanse your face.

3. *Wet your hair again. By rinsing off the surface dirt and letting your hair absorb the water, you will not need as much shampoo.* Pour shampoo into the palm of your hand. (The amount depends on the kind of shampoo you use. Some are more concentrated than others.) Rub your hands together to spread the shampoo and work up a lather. Distribute the shampoo all over your head instead of putting it in one spot and then trying to spread it. If you use a very concentrated shampoo, it

121

will be impossible to get it evenly spread unless you apply it this way.

4. *Gently massage your scalp and hair using fingertips, not your nails.* Spread your fingers apart and gently comb through your hair, detangling it as you go.

5. *Rinse.*

6. *Repeat shampoo application.* If you shampoo your hair every day, apply shampoo only once. You don't want to rob your hair of too many of its natural oils.

7. *Rinse again very thoroughly.* Do not skimp on this. It is the most important part of the process.

8. *Squeeze the water out of your hair, and apply a rinse or conditioner.* Let it work while you finish your bath (and shave your underarms and legs, if needed).

9. *Rinse your hair the final time.* Let the water run over it for a minute or two. Just before you get out, turn the water to cold if you can stand it! Your hair will have a hard gloss and you will feel invigorated!

10. *Wrap a towel around your head turban-style. Dry your face and body with another towel.* Apply your toner and moisturizer to your face and neck. Over a slightly moist body, apply your body lotion. Brush your teeth. Now, you are ready to comb out your hair.

11. *Never brush wet hair.* Brushing wet hair stretches the hair beyond its tensile strength, causing damage and breaking it. Use a wide tooth comb or a plastic vent brush with balls on the ends of the bristles. Start at the ends of the hair, and a section at a time, gently work your way up.

12. *Let your hair air dry as long as possible.* The wetter the hair, the longer the heat from the hair dryer has to be applied.

13. *If you do not have time for your hair to completely air dry, finish the process with your hair dryer.*

122

TIPS FOR BLOWING HAIR DRY

1. *Get as much excess water out of your hair as possible before beginning.* Wrap towel turban-style around freshly shampooed hair. Leave on five to ten minutes to allow the towel to absorb the moisture. *Do not* rub your hair vigorously with the towel. Let air dry until excess moisture is gone, or use your towel to blot your hair. For quick air drying, bend over at the waist and let your hair fall forward toward the floor. Open your fingers wide like a large comb and use them to shake the moisture out of your hair. Hair is weaker when wet, so remember to treat it very gently!

2. *With a wide tooth comb, part your hair into sections at the sides, back and top.* If your hair is very thick, you may want to make more sections. Pin each section with a large clip so the hair won't get in your way as you work.

3. *Starting with the sides, then back, and top last, brush and dry your hair in the direction opposite to the way it grows.* This will give a lot of volume to your hair. Use your vent brush for this step. Set the blow dryer on medium heat, not high, and with the dryer six to eight inches away from your hair, keep it moving at all times. You can damage your hair badly with a dryer. Some dryers get so hot you can cook an egg with them. Just think what that does to your hair.

4. *Now that your hair is dry, start working the style into it with a round bristle brush and your blow dryer.*

TIPS FOR OTHER HAIR EQUIPMENT AND PRODUCTS

CURLING IRON

A curling iron can be great in case of an emergency, but do not use it too often. Be sure yours has a Teflon nonstick coating, because they are less harmful to the hair than others. Hold the hair in the iron for only a few seconds so as not to burn or damage it.

HEAT ROLLERS

Heat rollers are great to use after you dry your hair if you want more curl. Again, be aware that they can be very damaging to your hair. Several products on the market (sprays and so on) are designed to protect your hair when heated equipment is used. If you need to use heat rollers, let your hair air dry as much as possible and use one of these special products. Let your hair completely cool before removing the curlers for the tightest curl.

CONDITIONERS

Deep-penetrating conditioners are a must for dry hair, for hair that has had a chemical product applied to it, and for hair that is blown dry or styled with heat rollers and/or a curling iron. Use weekly for damaged hair and twice a month for normal hair.

CREME RINSES

A creme rinse coats the hair strand but does not penetrate it. This helps to detangle the hair, making it easier to comb out. It is also protection against too frequent shampooing and heat equipment. If a creme rinse makes your hair oily or too soft, try applying it only to the ends of your hair.

QUESTIONS MOST OFTEN ASKED ABOUT HAIR

Participants of "The Teen I Want to Be" Workshops usually have lots of questions about hair and hair care. Here are some of them.

What does pH balance mean and why is it so important?

A. Your skin, including your scalp, has an acid mantle covering. The acid mantle is nature's way of helping to protect your skin from infection. Many things, such as poor diet, overexposure to the elements, and alkaline soaps and shampoos, can disturb this protective covering.

Measuring from zero to fourteen, dry skin is in the lower range, which is the acid side. Oily skin is on the higher range which is the alkaline side. The middle range is seven. Your goal is to bring your skin and scalp to nature's balance. Normal skin is slightly acid, at five or six.

You might want to go to the drugstore and buy a package of strips designed for testing pH and test your soaps and shampoos for yourself.

In addition to buying pH-balanced products that are reliable, you can restore the acid mantle to your skin very inexpensively by using something from your mom's kitchen—apple cider vinegar. For the final rinsing of your face, add one tablespoon of apple cider vinegar to a basin half filled with warm water. Rinse about twenty times with the mixture. Finish with cool water. For your hair, finish rinsing with one-half cup apple cider vinegar added to one quart of warm water. Rinse thoroughly with cool water to remove any vinegar odor.

Will perms, bleaches or color damage my hair?

A. Yes. Most of these products are harsh chemicals that are alkaline. They remove protein from the hair. Conditioners are a must if you use a chemical on your hair.

Is a creme rinse enough to keep my hair in good condition?

A. No. A creme rinse is good on a daily basis to detangle the hair, but you need to use a deep-penetrating conditioner periodically.

I want my hair to grow long. Should I still get it trimmed and if so, how often?

A. Yes, you should have your hair trimmed approximately every six weeks, even if you are letting it grow out. This will help to eliminate split ends. Have only a tiny bit removed until you reach the desired length.

How can I let my layers grow into a one length style such as the bob?

A. It takes a lot of determination to let layers grow out. Keep having the hair cut straight across at the neckline until the layers catch up.

How fast does hair grow?

A. The average hair growth is one-half to three-fourths inch per month. Of course, some people's hair grows faster than others.

In the summer time I swim a lot and my hair turns green. Is there anything I can do about it?

A. That is not an unusual problem. The chlorine in the swimming pool builds up on the hair causing it to look green. It will be very noticeable if you are a blonde. There are a couple of things you can do to help with this problem.
   1. Wet your hair and apply a conditioner before you go swimming. Wear a swimming cap, of course. This way you are actually helping your hair instead of damaging it while you swim.
   2. Buy a shampoo product especially designed for this hair problem. If your hair is very green, it may take several shampooings to get rid of it completely. Once you have solved the problem be sure to care for your hair as described in the first step.

Hair has been called a female's "crown of glory." Treasure your crown. Practice until you know how to care for it well and how to wear it beautifully. Make another dream come true. Have the best you hair and hair style.

Notes

- ♥ determine my face shape
- ♥ go to hair stylist

Tools

- ♥ hair brush
- ♥ plastic vent brush with ball on the end of the bristles
- ♥ wide tooth comb
- ♥ curling iron
- ♥ heat rollers
- ♥ hair accessories
    - barrettes
    - combs
    - headbands

Materials

- ♥ shampoo
- ♥ creme rinse
- ♥ conditioner
- ♥ file labeled HAIR for hair styles I like

CHAPTER TWELVE

the best me fashion image

♥ Clothes are a wonderful way to visually express something about yourself. A bridal gown, a uniform, and a tennis outfit all clearly tell us something about the wearer. In fact, what you have on this very minute is expressing something about you. Do you feel you always give the message that you would like? Or, should I ask, do you know the message you want to give? Think about it. Clothes can be fun as well as provide a necessary covering for your body. They are a means of creatively expressing your individuality.

STYLE—A MATTER OF PREFERENCE

Maybe you aren't sure what style you do prefer. Let me give you some definitions for each of these looks.

Trendy: The Latest Fashion Trend. These clothes can range from the dramatic to the bizarre. They have a short fashion cycle because the style changes each season. English designers have greatly influenced teens' trendy fashions in the past with such styles as "new wave" and "punk."

Which style do you prefer the most?

Preppy: The Ivy League Look. They are casual, comfortable, good quality clothes. Examples are the navy blazer, oxford cloth buttondown shirts, khaki skirts and pants, penny loafers, and dock siders.

TRENDY XX

PREPPY X

Romantic: The Very Feminine Look. Characteristics of this style are soft fabrics, full skirts, ruffles, lace, and pastel colors. The shoes are light in feeling such as the open toe or strippy sandal high heels.

ROMANTIC X

CLASSIC X

Classic: The Most Basic, Versatile Style. The lines are simple. They are less constructed and tailored than in the preppy style. The colors are basic. There are no extremes in design, therefore, the clothes have a long fashion life.

Try to train your eye to classify the style of clothes. Go through fashion magazines such as *Teen, Young Miss,* and *Seventeen* and identify the styles of the fashions. Cut out the pictures of the fashions that you especially like for yourself and keep them in a folder marked "Fashion." Ask yourself the following questions: What is the style? Why do I like this outfit? Where could I wear it? The more you train yourself to answer these questions, the more able you will be to shop wisely, express yourself creatively through fashion, and eliminate costly mistakes from your wardrobe.

Another valuable exercise to help you train your fashion eye is to go shopping—not to buy, just to look. It won't cost you a thing and you can have a great time. Go to the shops and departments in the stores that have the best merchandise. Study the clothes carefully. Why are they so much more expensive than other clothes? Feel the fabric, look at the construction, study the design. Train your eye on the very best. When you get ready to actually buy, you then will go to the price range you can afford. You will be able to detect the quality of workmanship as well as spot copies of the more expensive clothes.

Before you buy, you have a lot of homework to do! I am going to teach you step by step how to put your fashion image and wardrobe together. If you follow this information in the order in which it is given, you will have more outfits to wear on less money. It is tried and tested! You'll be surprised at how much you can put together from what you already have.

PUTTING YOUR FASHION IMAGE AND WARDROBE TOGETHER

Look over this list. What is different about the list and what most people do? Have you guessed it? Most people never bother with steps 1 through 5. When a new season comes, they get the urge to go shopping for new clothes. They call up a friend and off they go. They look at the new fashions and whatever they "just fall in love with," they buy. They spend all their money, and they still "don't have a thing to wear." They end up with a closet of misfits . . . nothing going together.

1. Understanding your clothing needs.
2. Inventorying your clothes.
3. Creatively making the most of what you have.
4. Effectively using what you have.
5. Determining new purchases.
6. Shopping.

In order to put your wardrobe together well, you will need to block out the time needed to do the job. You need to go through these six steps twice a year: at the beginning of the Spring/Summer season and at the beginning of the Fall/Winter season. If you do this, you will not need to shop at any other time. I know you are going to want to shop more because shopping is fun, but just think how great it would be if you knew your wardrobe was so well put together that whatever occasion arose you had the right thing to wear without having to panic and run out to the nearest shopping center to buy something. So block out a whole Saturday and get busy!

Start your day early in the morning with Step 1.

1. UNDERSTANDING YOUR CLOTHING NEEDS

List all of your activities, for example, school, church, tennis, dates, dressy parties, and weddings (even include sleeping—it requires a gown or pajamas).

Now go back and number the activities according to the number of clothes needed for the activity. The activity requiring the most changes of clothes would be number one while the activity requiring the least number of clothes would be your highest number. School will probably be your number one activity requiring the most outfits. An exception to that would be if you go to a school where you wear a uniform.

Now you know exactly what type of clothing you need and how much you need of each type. Many girls buy according to desire rather than need. For instance, you may spend all your money on blouses instead of buying the exact number you need simply because you love blouses. You then find that you have no money left for other items.

2. INVENTORYING YOUR CLOTHES

Get out all of the clothing you have, including accessories, for the season you are working on. You can wear many of your clothes year-round, such as jeans, some of your shirts and blouses, while other clothing, such as wool skirts, is definitely seasonal.

Sort the clothing into three groups: Group 1—clothes that you can wear (they fit and need nothing done to them); Group 2—clothes that need to be worked on; and Group 3—clothes that need to be gotten rid of.

Let's call the three groups The Okays, The Iffies, and The Gotta Goes.

As you go through this process, you will be aware that you have gotten a lot of wear out of some clothes, but others you might have worn only once or twice. Try to determine why you have worn some over and over and others hardly at all. Is it due to fit? Style? Fabric? Color? Comfort? Answering these questions will help you learn to buy things that will work for you. Eliminating mistakes in your wardrobe purchases can save you money.

Now that you have separated your clothes, let's get busy.

THE OKAYS

The goal is to get all of your clothing into this group. These clothes fit well, are in good condition, and do not need to be washed or dry cleaned.

Rule 1. *Never hang anything in your closet that needs to be washed, dry cleaned, pressed, or mended.*

If you hang a skirt with a safety pin in the waistband in your closet at the beginning of the season, you will pack it away that way at the end of the season. No one has time to sew on a button in the midst of rushing around to get somewhere. You may have the best intentions, but you just never get around to those things unless you do them up front.

THE IFFIES

These clothes need something done to them. You cannot or will not wear them the way they are. Some of them need to be mended, buttons sewn on, seams resewn, hems let down or shortened. Others will be clothes you simply do not like to wear, but you just can't get rid of them. You may remember that you really put the pressure on your mom to buy that dress for you and now you never wear it. You are sure she wouldn't be too happy if you gave it away.

With the first group—the ones that need to be mended—get out your needle and thread and get busy. Yes, *you* get out the needle and thread and get busy. It is important for *you* to know how to sew on buttons, mend clothes, and hem a skirt. If you do not know how, get your mom or grandmother to teach you. You might like to take a class to learn these basic, essential skills because you will need them for the rest of your life.

The second group—the clothes you don't like but can't get rid of—is another story. Study the garment and see if you could change anything to make it wearable for you. Let me give you a personal example. I made a dress for myself several years ago and enjoyed it for a season or two. I was then tired of the dress so I decided to cut it off and make a blouse out of it. I got a lot of wear out of the blouse. The next season I needed a scarf for a new outfit. I shopped and shopped and could never find one the right color. I remembered that I had saved the bottom part of the dress that I had cut off and it was the exact color that I needed. So, you guessed it! I made a scarf out of that dress bottom for my new outfit. Now really, you can't get much more mileage out of an outfit than that, can you?

Some other suggestions for you are to change a hemline, cut off the sleeves or restyle them, make a street-length dress out of a long dress. Study your clothes. See what changes you can make—and have fun doing it.

THE GOTTA GOES

I'll bet you have clothes hanging in your closet that have been too small for you for a long time. Right? I'll also bet you have clothes in your closet that you never wear and are never going to wear. Right? Get rid of them! There is nothing worse than to have a closet packed full of clothes and nothing to wear. Learn to keep your wardrobe pared down and simplified. Only those things that are in good condition, well maintained, suitable for you, and well coordinated should be in your closet.

Again, let me emphasize, get rid of those clothes you cannot wear. (I do suggest you check with your mom first, though, because your opinion of what you can't wear might be different from hers—and after all, your parents might have been the ones who paid for the clothes.) There are a number of different things you can do with your clothes. You can give them to someone else, you can swap outfits with someone, or you can donate them to charity or sell them at a yard sale. The important thing is that they be used, not just occupy space in a closet. The value of anything is its use.

Rule 2. *Never hang anything in your closet that you know you are not going to wear.*

Now that you have remade, repaired, or gotten rid of all of your problems, you only have okays in your closet.

3. CREATIVELY MAKING THE MOST OF WHAT YOU HAVE

Lay each garment across the bed or hang it on a coat rack and figure out how many different outfits you can come up with. Be as creative as you can be. Break up sets of clothes such as a matching skirt and jacket or pants and jacket. Work with them one piece at a time, mixing and matching with different pieces. Accessorize each outfit you put together. Learn to think in terms of the *total* look because the total look is what counts, not one outstanding piece.

Try to get looks from "low key" to "high key"—"low key" meaning very casual and "high key" meaning very dressy. Of course, the outfit will determine the range of looks you can give it. For example, you can put together many different looks, from casual to dressy, with an off-white skirt and jacket; on the other hand, you could never make a pink chiffon dress look casual/low key. (The pink chiffon dress would fit into only one category—dressy.)

Make a Wardrobe Chart for your closet, using this chart as a guide.

On the horizontal line list your activities (see page 137), starting with activity number one and listing in consecutive order.

In the vertical column, list each outfit that you put together, including accessories. If you lack an item of clothing or accessory to make the outfit complete (example, navy belt), note the missing item and draw a circle around it. Now, look across horizontally and put a check mark under each activity where you could wear the outfit. When you have finished charting your outfits, you will know many things about your wardrobe. You will know:

1. The number of outfits you have.
2. The number of outfits you have for each activity.
3. The activities for which you do not have as many outfits as you need.
4. The accessories or item of clothing you need in order to make a particular outfit complete.

Numbers three and four will be the basis of your shopping list later.

4. EFFECTIVELY USING WHAT YOU HAVE

Thumb tack or tape your Wardrobe Chart to the inside of your closet door. The important thing is to have this chart where you can refer to it often, otherwise, through habit, you will wear the same few outfits the same way each time.

♥ ♥ ♥ My Wardrobe Chart ♥ ♥ ♥

♥ outfits	activities										

The day that you work on your wardrobe is an excellent time to spring clean your room too. You already have everything pulled out of the closet and drawers so you might as well get double duty out of your time. That's called good time management!

Rule 3. *Hang your clothes in your closet in groups.*

For example, hang all skirts together, all blouses together, all slacks together, and so on. Yes, even hang your suit pieces separately.

Rule 4. *Hang your clothes in your closet in color families.*

Within each category (such as blouses), group in color families: all whites together, all reds, all blues, and so on.

Most people do not feel that they have enough closet space. Do you? You can try several ideas to better arrange your closet to be more effective and to stretch the space. A bulging, messy closet is not a very good incentive for putting yourself together in a well-groomed, fashionable way. In fact, a messy closet and room seem to carry over into everything that you do. Have you ever noticed? Get your room and closet in order, and you will be well on your way to getting your life in order.

So, get busy. You don't have to wait for the new year to make the resolution. Vacuum the closet from top to bottom, next the rest of the room, including under the bed. Now, of course, that may mean that you have to clean out from under the bed first. Go ahead, be ruthless in getting rid of all of those old magazines and other things that are just taking up space. With your new resource/file system, you won't be letting magazines stack up anymore anyway. Believe me, when you finish you are going to feel like a new person.

Look at your closet in a very critical (but constructive) way. How could it serve your needs better? If you need more space, analyze the situation and see if there is any way rods could be moved and additional ones added to double your space. Here is a drawing of a closet that might give you some ideas.

Several years ago, before we built our new home, we lived in a house that had closets with double sliding doors. Consequently, I could only get into half of the closet at a time. This was so frustrating because I wanted to be able to see all of my outfits at one time, and besides that I didn't have nearly enough space for my clothes. I would put them into the closet, nicely pressed, and get them out wrinkled because they were so packed together. With the desire for a better closet and some creative thinking, my husband and I came up with the idea in the drawing. He removed the sliding doors from the tracks and put the doors on hinges so they would open out and I could get into the whole closet at once. I found great-looking antique knobs to place on the doors. He built a row of shelves down the center for my shoes. Then he put a rod up high on one side for dresses and evening wear, and double rods on the other side of the shoe rack for blouses, skirts and slacks. He put hooks on the sides of the shoe rack for belts, jewelry, and other accessories. We covered the rods with pretty contact paper, and to make it smell nice and feminine I hung little bags of potpourri and sachet inside.

You can do your own remodeling of your closet as we did, or you can greatly simplify it by purchasing the new closet accessories for adding space. The new extenders designed for closets are wonderful.

5. DETERMINING NEW PURCHASES

Review your Wardrobe Chart. List the circled items; these are the items you need to make your outfits complete. Now review each activity. Do you have enough outfits for each activity? You might find that you do not have a dress appropriate for teas, weddings, or dressy events. You also might discover that you have more than enough clothes for some of your activities. List the needed outfits along with the circled items. These are the clothes you will want to purchase first. If there is any money left after you get the necessities, you can buy the fun things. This is a totally different way of doing things, isn't it? You are effectively using all that you already have before you begin to shop. Once you do it this way, you'll love it. You will have more great-looking outfits for less money than any other way you can put your wardrobe together!

Now let's talk about the most pleasing lines and colors for you because these things affect your clothing purchases too.

Have you ever had someone ask you if you had lost weight when your weight was exactly the same as before? Have you ever noticed that you look heavier in some outfits than in others? Line and/or color were probably responsible in both cases. When the lines of a garment interact with the lines of the total you, an optical illusion is created. This can work to your advantage as well as to your disadvantage. Knowing about line and color will help you to use them for your benefit.

CHARACTERISTICS OF LINE

| *Line* | | | *Characteristic* |

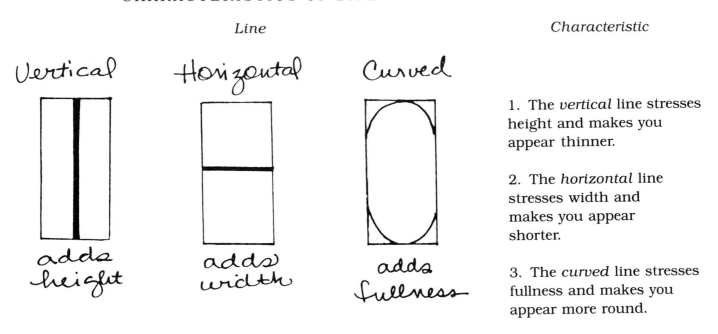

1. The *vertical* line stresses height and makes you appear thinner.

2. The *horizontal* line stresses width and makes you appear shorter.

3. The *curved* line stresses fullness and makes you appear more round.

Characteristic | *Line*

4. The *diagonal* line is a transitional line and adds neither height nor width. It disguises figure problems (an A-line skirt is an example).

5. The *asymmetrical* line fools the eye by shifting the center focal point. It disguises figure problems.

6. The *multiple* line adds both height and width. The wider the pleat or stripe, the more width is added to the body.

7. The *princess* line expands and nips in. It is ideal for the preteen figure because it gives the illusion of a bust line, hips, and a small waist.

8. When you repeat a line you emphasize its characteristic.

Study your figure. Review your figure chart. What are the best lines for your figure?

Diagonal

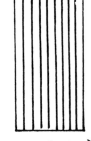

adds
interest
+
camouflages

Asymmetrical

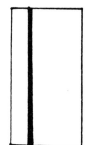

disguises

Multiple

adds
height
+
width

Princess

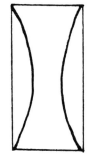

expands
+
nips in

CHARACTERISTICS OF COLOR

The Physical Properties of Color

1. *Hue* is the name of the color.

2. *Value* is the lightness or darkness of a color.

3. A *tint* is a color lighter than the color as it appears on the color wheel.

4. A *shade* is a color darker than the color as it appears on the color wheel.

5. *Intensity* is the brightness or dullness of a color.

Let's look at some examples. When the value of the hue red is light it is called pink, which is a tint. When the value of the hue red is dark, it is called garnet, which is a shade. The intensity of pink satin is bright. The intensity of garnet crepe is dull.

The Psychological Properties of Color

Color has tremendous power to influence certain responses.

1. Dark colors appear heavy, whereas light colors appear light in weight. That is the reason a light blouse with a dark skirt seems to be in better balance.

2. Certain values and intensities, such as pastel and bright colors, appear to be more youthful and active. Dark and dull colors appear to be quieter, more conservative, and older. A dark color, such as black, can appear very sophisticated.

3. Colors with a yellow undertone appear to be warm and colors with a blue undertone appear to be cool. Color Analysis is based on warm and cool undertones. (I will say more about this later.)

4. Light colors appear to advance. Dark colors appear to recede. Shiny colors (high intensity) appear to advance. Dull colors (low intensity) appear to recede. Warm colors appear to advance. Cool colors ap-

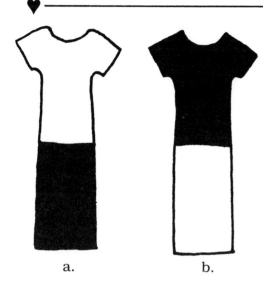

a.   b.

c.   d.

pear to recede. Advancing colors make you appear larger. Receding colors make you appear smaller. This principle plays a big part in make-up application as well as in fashion.

5. Color appears to make us feel certain ways:

Red—exciting and bold

Yellow—cheerful, warm, friendly, and rich

Blue—peaceful, cold, conservative, and quiet

Orange—vivacious, lively, and cheerful

Green—serene, friendly, and peaceful

Violet—regal, domineering, cold, and mysterious

Is your head spinning from all these definitions? Study them until you have a good understanding of their function. Then you will be able to apply the principles to many things in your life: putting your wardrobe together, decorating a room, applying make-up, painting a picture, or arranging flowers, just to name a few things you can do in which colors play an important part.

LINE AND COLOR TEST

Let's test your knowledge now. How would each outfit on the left affect the figure: a. _____ b. _____ c. _____ d. _____

Which pair of shoes would make the feet appear smaller:

a. white pair ___? or black pair ___?

b. black suede pair ___? or black patent pair ___?

(See answers at the end of this chapter.)

DETERMINING YOUR MOST BECOMING COLORS

Color does make a difference in your appearance. Have you ever had someone say to you, "You don't look like you feel well today"? You

144

felt perfectly well until you heard that! If that is the case, you were probably wearing a color that made you look unhealthy. At other times you have probably had people say to you, "Wow! You look great," and you had not done anything any different to yourself to warrant such an enthusiastic compliment. Again, color was probably the cause. You were probably wearing colors that made your skin look clear and vibrant and brought out the highlights in your hair.

Color Analysis, the determining of your best colors, has become tremendously popular over the past few years. It isn't anything new. (It has been around as long as the theory of color has.) The newness is the way in which Color Analysis is presented so that anyone can understand it and apply it.

The theory behind Color Analysis is that everyone's coloring is either warm or cool, warm meaning a yellow undertone and cool meaning a blue undertone. The skin is the primary way to determine coloring, with hair next, and eyes last. Within the two categories, warm and cool, there is a wide range of value and intensity of personal coloring. For example, I am cool in my color undertone. I have two sisters and they happen to be cool too. They are blonde and blue eyed, while I have dark brown hair and eyes. The colors that look best on me are too overpowering for them, while the colors that look best on them weaken my coloring. This kind of range of value and intensity of coloring within the two color undertones make it necessary to establish categories.

The most popular names of the four categories are taken from nature. They are Spring, Summer, Autumn, and Winter. Spring and Autumn are the warm colors, and Summer and Winter are the cool colors. The colors that are best for you correspond with the colors of a particular season. I am a Winter; my two sisters are Summers.

THE WARM SEASONS

Spring

Spring is the warm, bright season. Spring persons are often the most youthful and vibrant looking of the seasons. They never seem to age. They have ivory skin which looks like peaches and cream. They blush easily, and they usually have rosy cheeks.

Their hair is a golden blonde, light red, or light brown with golden highlights. Spring's eyes are clear and bright. The eye color may be blue, blue green, green, or a light brown with yellow in it.

Spring's colors are clear and bright with a warm undertone. The blonde Spring looks wonderful in creams and ivory from head to toe. Add a strand of pearls and she looks like a golden girl.

Autumn

Autumn is the warm, muted season. Autumn people have rich earthy coloring just like the season they are named after. Their skin has a golden tone to it. Many times the Autumn person will have freckles, which have a golden tone to them too. The skin tone can have a flushed red look.

Their hair is usually red or brown with red or golden highlights. Most Autumns have brown eyes. Other eye colors are in the olive family and the turquoise family. Gold flecks usually appear in all of the eye colors.

Autumns wear both bright and rich earthy tone colors. Their best color family is gold.

THE COOL SEASONS

Summer

Summer is the cool, muted season. Summer people have translucent, pale pink skin. Their skin is usually thin and does not suntan well; it burns instead. The hair is blonde or light brown with an ash undertone. Many Summers were towheads as children, but as adults their hair turned dark.

The eye color is most often blue, sometimes hazel, and least frequently a soft brown. The eye color is not as clear as that of Spring. The iris may be rimmed with gray. Summers look beautiful in pale, muted colors in harmony with their coloring. Strong colors are too overpowering for them. The blue family is Summer's best!

Winter

Winter is the cool, bright season. The Winter person has the strongest coloring of any of the seasons, giving her, many times, a dramatic look. There are more Winter people than any of the other seasons. The light-skinned Winter has a blue undertone that may appear pinkish or olive. There is a lot of contrast between the skin tone and the hair and eye coloring. The dark-skinned Winter has a bluish undertone to the skin. Most blacks and orientals are Winters. The hair color of Winter in the teen years is usually dark brown with red highlights, black with a bluish or smoke cast, or a white blonde.

The eye color may be a reddish brown, black brown, blue gray, blue violet, green, grayish green, or hazel. Brown eyes are the most predominant. Many times the iris has a gray ring around it.

Winters look great in bright, contrasting colors, because they emphasize the Winter's own coloring. Black and white are especially good on them.

147

When trying to determine your season, keep these pointers in mind.

When the color is right for you,

- The viewer's eye will be drawn to your face, not to the color. You will wear the color instead of the color's wearing you.
- Your skin, hair, and eye coloring will be enhanced and emphasized. Your skin will appear clearer.
- People will tend to compliment *you* when you are wearing the right color.

When the color is wrong for you,

- The viewer's eye will be drawn to the color you are wearing.
- Your skin, hair, and eye coloring will be weakened. They will not look as vibrant as when you are wearing the right colors. Flaws in your skin will be emphasized.
- People will tend to compliment what you are wearing instead of *you*.

If you are still unsure about your coloring, have your color professionally analyzed to determine your color season. If you have determined your coloring, you may want to order a Shopper's Guide, which includes swatches of the colors in your color season. (See the order form on page 192.) You will need the actual swatches of color for your shopping trips. You might think you can remember color, but most people can't. Your Shopper's Guide will enable you to know if an outfit is your color or not.

Once you know your color palette, you will realize that you have some clothes in your wardrobe that are not in your best colors. Don't panic and throw them away. Try to wear the outfit with one of *your* colors close to your face. For instance, you may have a jacket that is a color not in your palette. Simply wear it with a blouse in one of your best colors. Then as you make new purchases, buy only in your color palette. Phase out the wrong colors and replace them with your colors. This will take several years, but it will be worth the effort. When you have only your colors in your wardrobe, you will see how fabulous it is. Everything in your wardrobe will work together. You will also have the added bonus of knowing you look great!

6. SHOPPING

The best times of the year to go shopping are at the beginning of the Spring/Summer season and at the beginning of the Fall/Winter season before all of the merchandise is picked over. Block out plenty of time during these two periods of the year to get your wardrobe in tiptop shape. If you wait until you need an outfit, you will rush out and spend more money on it than you intended to spend, and you may even have to take something you don't particularly like.

Study the fashion magazines. Go to the seasonal fashion shows. Observe how the mannequins are put together in the better department stores and shops. Know what's going on in fashion.

Your shopping list should be complete in details before you begin. Include the following information:

1. Amount of clothing allowance
2. Articles of clothing needed
3. Style of each needed article
4. Best line for your figure for each needed garment
5. Color of each piece of clothing

With your shopping list and your Shopper's Guide in hand, you are ready to go! I suggest that you don't take a friend along with you. You have a very clear idea of what you want to accomplish, and it's going to take hard work and concentration for you to find exactly what you need

149

in your price range. Your friend will probably still be looking at clothes from an emotional standpoint rather than from a well-thought-out plan. She might take you off track by her excitement over an outfit that she just loves! On the other hand, your mom would be great to have along. She will probably have been involved in what you are doing already. She might be the one responsible for your clothing allowance, and she could have helped make the decisions about your clothes when you cleaned out your closet. On your shopping trip you could benefit from your mom's experience. Pay close attention to what she says. At the same time, you make as many decisions as you can. This is the only way you can develop your sense of style and know-how.

Just as your friends can lead you away from your goal, so can a salesperson. Build sales resistance. Don't be taken in by flattery. Stay with your goal. (Salespeople can be a big help too, if they understand your goal!)

As you look in the shops, eliminate everything that is not in your color palette. This will save you a lot of time because you won't have to go through everything on the racks.

Buy clothes and accessories in your color palette only. If you buy only your colors, you ensure that everything will be flattering to you and that everything will go together.

The very best buys are separates. Buy these in a basic, classic style and in a neutral or basic color from your color palette. You will be able to mix and match the separates. Put your bright and pastel colors in blouses, sweaters, and accessories.

Update your wardrobe with accessories. Give your outfits the newest look with the accessories you put with them. Buy the best quality basic clothes you can afford. Then look for inexpensive ac-

150

cessory items. By buying the inexpensive "fad" items, you can afford not to wear them next season when they have gone out of style.

THE FASHIONABLE YOU

Once you have taken the time to put your wardrobe together the way you have just learned, you will never be without "anything to wear." You will always be dressed appropriately for any occasion. You will have a new confidence about yourself, and you will look your absolutely stunning best!

ANSWERS TO LINE AND COLOR TEST (p. 144):

Outfits

a. The top will appear larger, the bottom smaller. The figure is shortened because the garment has a horizontal line across the body and contrasting colors.
b. The top will appear smaller, the bottom larger. The figure is shortened because the garment has a horizontal line across the body and contrasting colors.
c. The vertical lines stress height making the figure appear taller. Light panels on the sides make the figure appear fuller.
d. The vertical lines stress height making the figure appear taller. Dark panels on the sides make the figure appear smaller.

Shoes

a. The black pair. Again, dark colors recede making the foot look smaller.
b. The black suede pair. Dull colors (low intensity) recede making the foot look smaller.

Notes

- ♥ inventory my clothes
- ♥ fill in my Wardrobe Chart
- ♥ work on my shopping list
- ♥ determine my color undertone
- ♥ buy clothes in my color palette only!

Materials

- ♥ file folder labeled FASHION for pictures of accessories & fashions I like
- ♥ color swatches for my season

CHAPTER THIRTEEN

the best me lingerie

♥ Going braless is out. It never was really in! Wearing a bra is beneficial to your health. Your doctor will agree that good support is important to keep the breast muscles from stretching and sagging, causing the breasts to lose firmness and shape.

A PROPER FITTING BRA

Do you know how to buy the correct size bra? According to bra manufacturers, 75 per cent of females wear bras that do not fit properly. Don't guess at your size. Learn how to determine the size and style best for you. I guarantee you will look much better in your clothes and be healthier in the process.

Get out your trusty old tape measure. Stand up straight and place the tape measure just under your bust to determine your *bra size*. If the measurement is an odd number, such as 33, add 1 inch to the number so that you have an even number (33 + 1 = 34 bra size). To determine the *cup size,* measure over the fullest part of your bust. If the measurement of the bust is up to 1 inch larger than your bra size, you wear an AA cup. If it is 1 to 2 inches larger than your bra size, you wear an A cup. If it is 2 to 3 inches larger, you wear a B cup. If it is 3 to 4 inches larger, you wear a C cup, and so on. AAA is the smallest cup size and DDD is the largest cup size that bras come in.

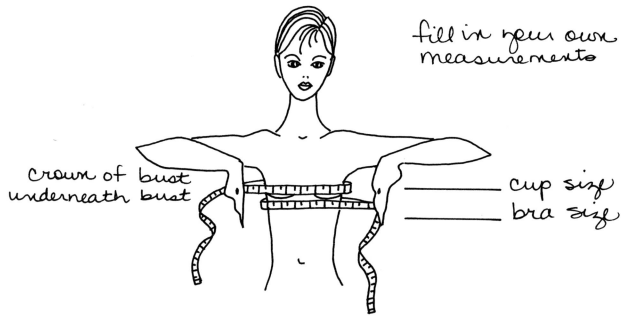

fill in your own measurements

crown of bust
underneath bust

cup size
bra size

Here are some questions to keep in mind when you buy your next bra.

Is the bra too tight? Look for bulges over the bra.

Do the cups wrinkle? Cup wrinkles usually mean that the cup size is too small.

154

Do you need to tighten the straps to make it fit? The straps of the bra have nothing to do with the fit. The support of the bra comes from the construction underneath the cups. Try this test. Drop one strap off your shoulder and see if you still have good support. If not, the bra is not the correct size.

Does the bra ride up in the back? When a bra rides up in the back, it is usually a result of the straps being too tight. If you need to tighten the straps for support, you have the wrong size bra.

If you still don't feel comfortable with your bra selection, get the help of a professional fitter. The better department stores and lingerie shops provide this service at no cost. Take advantage of it! Pick up the phone and make an appointment.

BRA WARDROBE

In addition to fit, you will want to consider the different kinds of bras you need for your wardrobe.

1. *Smooth-cupped bra.* Wear with sweaters and knit fabric shirts and dresses. Seamed or lacy bras will show through your outfit.

2. *Strapless bra.* Wear with dresses and tops that have very narrow straps over the shoulders or have wide necklines. Nothing looks worse than someone's bra straps showing.

Check the back of your dress or top at the neckline. Does the bra show in the back? If it barely shows, a strapless bra can be slightly pushed down in the back. But if the back neckline is very low, you will need a special bra designed for backless dresses.

3. *Sports bra.* Wear when jogging, playing tennis, or participating in any active sport. Constant bouncing of the breasts can be very damaging to the muscles and tissue. (Pay particular attention to this if

155

you are full busted.) The sports bra should have wide straps for good support, seamless cups, and padded fasteners so your body is not rubbed in any way.

Good bras are expensive, but if you take good care of them, they will last a long time. Wash your bras with a mild detergent by hand or on the gentle cycle in your washing machine. (I have a mesh bag that I put mine in for added protection when I wash them in the washing machine.) The dryer will damage your bras, so let them air dry.

Don't let a bra rob you of your poise. When you think your bra *might* show, you will constantly be adjusting and fidgeting with your clothing. Take the time to make sure your undergarments are correct for what you are wearing.

SLIPS

Have you ever gone without a slip and had your clothes cling to you all day? If you have, you know how uncomfortable it is to spend the entire day pulling your dress or skirt away from your body and legs. A slip keeps that from happening. Or have your left home feeling perfectly confident about yourself only to discover that once you stepped into the bright daylight someone could see right through your clothes? How embarrassing! You needed to have a slip on.

Slips come in two styles, a full slip and a half-slip. A full slip is needed only when the top part of your outfit is sheer enough to show your bra. Even then you can wear a half-slip and a camisole. (I think half-slips are the most comfortable.) The slip size is determined by your waist size unless you have very full hips.

With the different lengths of skirts in style now, you will probably need three different lengths of slips. Two beige and one white in regular length for your standard-length clothes, one tall length for your longer

156

clothes, and one full-length for your full-length clothes should cover all your slip needs. If you wear a lot of dark colors, you might want to include a black or navy half-slip, too. (Those of you who are five nine or over will want to buy three tall size half-slips, and you may need to cut off a full-length slip for your longer clothes in order to get one long enough.) Remember, the length of your slip is *very* important.

PANTIES

The biggest mistake teens make with panties is buying bikini styles that are too small or wearing ones they have outgrown. Panties that are too small cause unsightly bulges. It is especially noticeable when the too-tight panties are worn under too-tight jeans or slacks. Yuk! Besides, it isn't good for your health because it cuts off circulation. Check the chart on the package to determine your correct size. You can try the new pair on over your panties to be sure they fit. I think the best choice is a plain style in beige or white with a cotton crotch.

PANTYHOSE

Sandalfoot hose are the best buy since you can wear them with any type shoe. A reinforced toe or heel ruins the total look when worn with a sandal or open-toe shoe. These little things determine whether or not you'll have a polished look. If you wear heavier, closed-in shoes or boots often, you will need the reinforced toe for them. Just be sure you don't get lax and wear the wrong kind of hose with your shoes.

Be careful with your hose. Learn how to take care of them. Here are a few tips:
• Be sure you have no jagged fingernails or toenails to cause snags.
• Don't snag your hose with your jewelry.

157

- To put your hose on, sit down and carefully gather one leg of your hose down to the foot and slip it onto your toe and then your heel. Repeat this with the other foot. Alternate pulling the legs up and smoothing them out. Adjust the waistband.
- Hand wash your pantyhose with a mild detergent and rinse thoroughly. Absorb the excess water in a towel by gently squeezing. Air dry. Wash after each day's wearing.

Colored hose go in and out of fashion from year to year. Regardless of the fashion, you will need several pairs of neutral-colored pantyhose in your wardrobe.

LINGERIE WARDROBE

	Starter Wardrobe	Basic Wardrobe
• Beige-colored bras with smooth cups	2	3
• White bra	—	1
• Strapless bra	1	1
• Navy or black bra (if you wear dark colors often)	—	1
• Sports bras (depending on how often you participate in sports)	1	2
• Beige colored half-slips	2	3
• Tall length half-slip for longer clothes	1	1
• Full-length slip	1	1
• Dark half-slip (optional)	—	1
• Beige-colored camisole	—	1
• Beige-colored panties	4	7
• Neutral-colored sandalfoot pantyhose	2	3
• Reinforced toe and heel pantyhose	as needed	
• Colored pantyhose when in fashion	as needed	

Notes

- ♥ determine my sizes
- ♥ work on my basic lingerie wardrobe

the best me skin care

♥ Beautiful skin does not begin with the right make-up. It begins with diet, exercise, and the way you feel about yourself. Your skin is a good indicator of what's going on with you—inside and out. Stress, emotional turmoil, junk foods, too little water, and a lethargic, lazy body play havoc with your complexion. Vigorous exercise is the best facial you can give yourself. It brings the blood to the face, stimulating and toning it. Drinking at least eight glasses of water daily helps toward the prevention of acne. It is also the best moisturizer for the skin because it hydrates the skin from within. Review the sections of the book concerning each of these areas. Make any changes necessary to bring yourself to optimal health in every way.

Now that you have everything in order, let's talk about skin care. There are four basic steps to good skin care:
1. Cleansing
2. Toning
3. Moisturizing
4. Exfoliating (removing the dead cells)

TYPE OF SKIN

Before determining the method and products you will use for your four-step skin care program, you need to know what kind of skin you have and some of its characteristics.

My skin type is

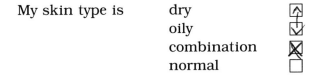

dry

oily

combination

normal

If you are not quite sure which yours is, perhaps the following descriptions will help you to decide.

Dry skin is very fine in texture. It feels tight and drawn. After you wash your face with soap and water, your face feels as if it will crack if you smile. It is rough and scaly, especially in the winter. This type of skin sunburns easily, and as you get older, it tends to wrinkle easily. Most teens have very active oil glands because of body changes, so you probably do not have this skin type. Since the skin has a tendency to become drier with age, you may develop dry skin as you get older (past thirty).

Oily skin is coarse in texture with enlarged pores. Oil accumulates in the pores causing blackheads and blemishes. Your face gets shiny during the day. If you have very oily skin and wear a make-up foundation, by the end of the day it feels like your make-up is going to slide off. The oil may cause your make-up to turn yellow. During the teen years the oil glands are very active; therefore, you just might fit into this category.

Combination skin is exactly what it says . . . a combination of two skin types. Certain areas may be dry or normal and other areas oily. The

161

most common combination is to have an oily forehead, nose, and chin (called the "T" zone) with dry or normal skin in the other areas of the face.

Normal skin is smooth and clear, neither oily nor dry. The texture is fine and even, with no noticeable pores. If you still can't decide which skin type you have, you probably have normal.

The most important thing to do to care for your skin is to keep it clean. Cleanse it morning and night—yes, twice a day without fail! It doesn't matter how tired you are, don't ever go to bed without first cleansing your face. I can't stress this too much. Dirt, oil, grime, and make-up left on the face overnight cause the pores to clog and blemishes as well as whiteheads and/or blackheads to appear. Clean! Clean! Clean! Don't skip the morning cleansing either. Even though the only thing you have done is sleep (and with a clean face too), you still need to cleanse your face because the glands have secreted oil, and your face has been exposed to bacteria and pollutants in the air.

Follow the skin care routine I've described for your particular skin type. It takes twenty-one days of repetition for something to become a habit. Set a goal to properly care for your skin for twenty-one days, and you are well on your way to establishing a habit that will benefit you enormously for the rest of your life.

CARE FOR DRY SKIN

MORNING

1. Wash your face and neck with a mild soap and warm water (not hot), using your fingertips instead of a cloth. Rinse your face in warm running water twenty times (this takes about one minute of rinsing).

Rinse the last couple of times with cool water. Blot the water off your face with a soft towel.

2. Tone with an alcohol-free freshener. (Be sure to check the ingredients on the freshener bottle so as to avoid alcohol. It is too drying for your skin type.) Apply freshener to a cotton ball and rub over your face and neck. Continue to reapply until there is no dirt left on the cotton ball.

3. Apply a moisturizer formulated for dry skin. If you have very dry skin you may want to skip the freshener in the morning and apply your moisturizer over a damp face and neck.

NIGHT

1. If you wear make-up, remove your make-up with a cleansing liquid, cream, or a natural cold-pressed oil instead of soap. You can buy a natural cold-pressed oil at a health food store. (Your mom may already have some that she uses for cooking.) Remove the cleanser with a warm washcloth.

If you do not wear make-up, you can use either the cleansing cream or soap, according to your preference.

2. Repeat morning procedure Step 2.

3. You may want to use a richer moisturizer called a "night cream." Apply it liberally, and just before getting into bed, blot your face with a tissue to remove the excess. You don't want to wake up in the morning with greasy hair and a grease-stained pillow.

CARE FOR OILY SKIN

MORNING

1. Wash your face with a mild soap (or an antiacne soap if you have pimples). Work up plenty of lather with your hands, and using your

fingertips, massage thoroughly. Rinse your face in warm running water twenty times, about one minute. Rinse the last couple of times with cool water. Blot the water off your face with a soft towel.

2. Tone with an astringent. This product has alcohol in it, and it will tighten and refine the pores as well as remove any dirt or oil that still remains on the skin. Apply with a cotton ball until no trace of dirt is left on the cotton ball.

3. If your skin is excessively oily, you should not apply a moisturizer. On very oily skin, a moisturizer can clog the pores and cause the skin to break out. Around your eyes and mouth and on the ears and neck, you may need to apply a moisturizer.

NIGHT

1. If you wear make-up, remove it with a cleansing liquid or cream or a cold-pressed oil. Follow procedure with soap and water.

2. Repeat Step 2 for morning.

3. Same as Step 3 for morning.

CARE FOR COMBINATION SKIN

MORNING

1. Wash your face with a mild soap and warm water, using your fingertips instead of a cloth. Rinse your face in warm running water twenty times. Rinse the last couple of times with cool water. Blot the water off your face with a soft towel.

2. Tone dry areas with an alcohol-free freshener. Use an astringent in the "T" zone. Apply with a cotton ball until no trace of dirt is left on the cotton ball.

3. Apply a moisturizer to the dry areas only.

NIGHT

1. If you wear make-up, remove it with a cleansing liquid, cream, or a natural cold-pressed oil. If you do not wear make-up, you can use either the cleansing cream or soap, according to your preference.

2. Repeat morning procedure Step 2.

3. Moisturize your skin. You may want to use a richer moisturizer (a night cream) in the dry areas and a regular moisturizer in the "T" zone.

CARE FOR NORMAL SKIN

1., 2., 3. Treat with same procedure as for Dry Skin.

4. EXFOLIATING (REMOVAL OF DEAD CELLS)

On a weekly basis, after cleansing your face at night, omit Step 2 (freshener or astringent) and use either a scrub or masque (not both) on your face. Follow with Step 3 to moisturize.

The scrub or masque removes dry, dead cells and refines the pores. If you have oily skin, you would benefit by using both a scrub and a masque once a week. A cleansing sponge, which exfoliates, is also good for oily skin. Use it with an antiseptic cleanser. Oily skin should be kept very clean so that pores do not clog and get infected. You can buy a product to exfoliate and deep cleanse your face suited for your particular skin type or you can make your own.

ITEMS YOU CAN USE FOR SCRUBS

You can use cornmeal, oatmeal, or almond meal (made by putting almonds in the blender) as a scrub. Apply the meal to your moist face, and gently work the product in a circular motion, avoiding the eye area and mouth. Rinse thoroughly. Apply moisturizer.

A MASQUE YOU CAN MAKE AT HOME

Make a paste with equal parts honey and oatmeal, then add one beaten egg. Apply the masque evenly all over your face, avoiding your eyes and mouth. Let set for ten to twenty minutes. (If you purchase a commercially made masque, carefully read all the directions about how to use it and about how long to leave it on.) Rinse off thoroughly. Apply moisturizer.

If you have the time, steam your face before you begin. You can do this by applying a washcloth, dipped in hot water and wrung out, to your face several times or by filling your basin with boiling water and holding your face over the steam, using a towel over your head to create a tent for catching the steam. Apply the masque. Stretch out on a slant board and give the masque time to dry thoroughly. Rinse well and apply moisturizer.

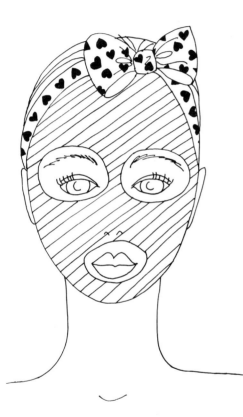

TIPS FOR BEAUTIFUL SKIN AND ACNE PREVENTION

1. Eat well-balanced meals based on the Basic Four food groups.
2. Take a multi-vitamin and mineral supplement daily.
3. Exercise daily.
4. Drink at least eight glasses of water daily.
5. Cleanse, tone, and moisturize your face twice daily.
6. Use a scrub and/or masque weekly.
7. Keep your hands off your face.
8. Do not squeeze blemishes, blackheads, or whiteheads.
9. Visit a dermatologist if you have a severe skin problem.
10. Do not overexpose your skin to the sun.
11. Wear a sunscreen when in the sun.
12. Get plenty of sleep.

Notes

♥ eat properly
♥ take a multi-vitamin
♥ drink plenty of water

Tools

♥ complexion sponge

Materials

♥ cleanser toner moisturizer
♥ scrubb
♥ masque

YOUR BEAUTIFUL SKIN IS SHOWING

You will be greatly rewarded for your diligence in caring for your skin. These habits will benefit you the rest of your life, and beautiful, vibrant skin will be yours!

CHAPTER FIFTEEN

the best me make-up

♥ Remember how you loved to get into your mom's make-up when you were little? Females of all ages love make-up. They are always ready to experiment, hoping to come up with a look that shows them at their gorgeous best. Interestingly enough, the best way to achieve this, with the least effort, is to have your skin in excellent condition before you begin. The more skin problems you have, the more difficult your make-up application will be.

HOW OLD SHOULD I BE?

I'm constantly asked, "How old should a girl be before she starts wearing make-up?" There is no pat answer to that question. Some girls want to wear make-up at a very early age, but others do not. Some wear very little all the way through high school and college. I feel that the fifth, sixth, and seventh grades are too early for a girl to wear eyeshadow, eyeliner, mascara, and the "works."

Does your mother think you are too young to wear make-up? Does she think you wear too much make-up? Listen to her. Talk about it. She is for you, not against you, so take her advice. Jodi started wearing a lip gloss and blush when she was fifteen. She had not wanted to wear make-up sooner, and I'm glad. Since starting to college, she wears more make-up, although her brothers still like her better without it. Guys don't seem to like girls to wear make-up as much as girls seem to like to wear it.

MAKE-UP APPLICATION RULES

Regardless of whether you are dreaming about wearing make-up someday, getting ready to start wearing it, or already wearing it, you need to learn a couple of basic rules about make-up application.

Rule 1. It is not the number of products you use that determines whether you look too made up or natural. It is the amount you apply and how well you apply it. You can wear only lipstick and look too made up, whereas you can wear ten products and look natural. Therefore, apply make-up sparingly, and after each product application, check in a magnifying mirror to be sure you have applied it evenly and accurately.

Rule 2. Make-up application is based on the theory that "light advances and dark recedes." In other words, a light color on an area will seem to bring the area forward, and a dark color will seem to push the area back. Study your face before you begin your make-up. Know what you want to accomplish. On the areas you want to lighten or bring forward, use a light-colored product. On the areas you want to push back, use a dark color.

With Rule 2 in mind, study your face carefully. Tie your hair back from your face with a ribbon. Look in the mirror. Notice the shape of your face, your cheekbones, eyebrows, the shape of your eyes, the amount of space between your eyes, your lips, your skin tone, and so on. If you had a head and shoulder photograph made of yourself when you were determining your face shape (see "Hair Styles," page 114), it will be very helpful now too. Get the photograph and some tracing paper.

Draw a line down the center of your face. Compare each side. You will notice the shapes of the eyebrows, eyes, nostrils, and lips are different. Decide which side of your face you think is the most pleasing, and when you apply make-up, make the less pleasing side look like the better side.

STEP BY STEP MAKE-UP APPLICATION

I am going to teach you step by step how to do a complete make-up job. Apply in the order that I have here. If you do not wish to do one of the steps, skip it and go to the next one.

1. CLEANSE   2. TONE   3. MOISTURIZE

Review Chapter 14 and follow procedure for your skin type.

4. FOUNDATION

Foundations come in many different forms, all the way from a wash to a pancake type. The thinner the product, the lighter the coverage; the thicker the product, the heavier the coverage. You want to select the thinnest product that will give you the maximum coverage you need. Your skin should still look natural after you apply the foundation. Too thick a foundation makes you look like you are wearing a mask.

In addition to the degree of coverage, you need to consider your skin type when selecting the correct product. Read the label on the bottle to know if it is water based (no oil), oil controlled (5 to 10 per cent oil), or oil based (up to 30 per cent oil). For *normal* or *dry skin*, the oil-based foundation works well. A water-based product on normal or dry skin causes it to look chalky and flaky. *Oily skin* needs the water-based or oil-controlled product. Another good product for oily skin with large pores is called a "pore minimizer." It has an astringent base, is very thin, and goes on like a wash, but the coverage is excellent.

Choosing the correct shade of foundation is most important. It should be as close to your own skin color as possible. Your skin either has a blue undertone or a yellow undertone. If you have been color analyzed, you know whether you are cool (blue) or warm (yellow). Foundations are rose beige undertoned (blue) and yellow beige undertoned (yellow). Ask the salesperson at the cosmetic counter for a foundation with the same undertone as your skin. Test it on your make-up—free face just above the jawline on your cheek. When it's blended, you should hardly be able to see it. If it is too dark or too light, try another shade.

Your work is a little harder if you don't know your undertone. In that case, you will have to try both the warm and cool tones of foundation to see which one is closer to your skin. Many people test foundation on the inside of their wrists. I do not recommend this because there can be a big difference in the shade on your wrist and the shade on your face (although the undertone will be the same).

Once you have selected the correct color, working with a well-lighted mirror, apply the foundation sparingly. With your fingertips place a dot of foundation on your forehead, nose, and chin and two dots on each cheek. Blend upward and out toward your hairline. Blend onto your lips (this will help your lipstick stay on longer). Do not apply foundation to your neck because it will ruin your clothes. Look into the magnifying side of your mirror for any skipped places or mistakes. Make sure your foundation is blended well at the jawline so you do not see a line where the foundation stops.

You can apply foundation with a damp make-up sponge as well as with your fingers. Using a sponge gives a sheer coverage, but it also uses more foundation and takes a little longer to apply. Try both ways to see which you prefer.

5. CONCEALER

A concealer is a product used to cover up dark circles under the eyes, blemishes, small scars and dark spots (but *not* freckles). This product needs to be several shades lighter than your foundation. It comes in several forms: cream cake, tube (looks like a lipstick), and wand. You can apply it either before or after you apply your foundation. (Most people I have noticed rub the concealer away when they apply it before the foundation.) I prefer to apply it on top of my foundation and gently blend it, using light pats with my middle finger. Be careful around the eye area, do not pull and tug the skin when you apply the concealer. By using your middle finger, you will use very light pressure for blending. Remember to check the magnifying side of your mirror to see if you have applied the concealer correctly and only on the needed area. You want it to be light enough to cover the area but not so light that you look like a panda bear with big white circles around your eyes.

6. LOOSE, TRANSLUCENT FACE POWDER

Loose, translucent face powder is very sheer. It usually comes in light, medium, and dark shades although it does not add any color to

172

your face. In fact, if your skin is very light, you can use baby powder in an emergency. Apply with a fresh cotton ball or a face powder brush. Do not use the puff that comes with the powder. It will absorb the oil from your skin, and it will become unsanitary. (This is particularly important if you have oily, blemished skin.) Dip the fresh cotton ball or brush into the powder, shake off the excess, then dust your face all over, including your lips, with the powder. Brush in downward strokes, the direction your facial hairs grow, so that you do not create a fuzz. Brush over your face again. This takes away the shine from your face, gives you a beautiful sheen, and sets your make-up. A pressed powder compact is handy to carry in your purse for touchups during the day but is not the kind to use when you do your make-up. It has oil in it and will clog your pores.

7. BLUSH

A blush applied well can make your face come alive. Applied too heavily, it can make you look like a clown, so be careful. You will probably want to start using a blush before you start using a foundation or a concealer. (Blush and a lip gloss are usually the first cosmetics a girl wears.) Even after you have started wearing complete make-up, you will have some days when you don't want to go to all the trouble. Just put on some blush and you'll look alive. Blushes come in gels, creams, and powders. The powder is the easiest to use, and it is the only one that goes on after the loose, translucent face powder. The gels and creams go on before. If you apply a powder blush to a freshly moisturized face, you may get streaks. Loose, translucent powder will prevent the streaking.

The color of the blush is important. Blushes as well as foundations come in warm or cool undertones. The warm blushes have an orange

173

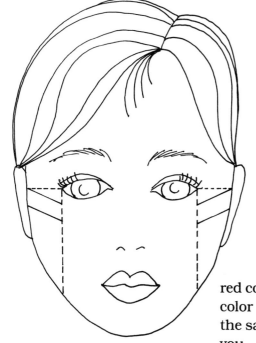

① Draw an imaginary line from the corner of the eye down.

② Find cheekbone and apply blush on cheekbone.

red color such as peach or russet, while the cool blushes have a blue red color such as rose or burgundy. Be sure the undertone of the blush is the same as the undertone of your skin. A blush should look natural on you—just as though blood had rushed to your cheeks.

To apply, look in the mirror and draw imaginary lines straight down from the outside corners of both eyes. Now find your cheekbones. Starting at the imaginary line you have drawn and on your cheekbone, apply the blush, feathering it out into the hair line. Do not come closer in than the corner of your eye or lower than the end of your nose. Try not to put the blush too close to your eye. A little, wedge-shaped make-up sponge works well for blending the blush.

174

8. EYEBROWS

Eyebrows can make you look surprised, depressed, or a lot of other strange ways when you try to create a look totally different from your own natural one. Thanks to Brooke Shields, natural brows are popular again. A number of years ago, the fashion was to have pencil-thin brows. What a lot of plucking that took! I'm thankful that's out!

To know the best shape for your eyebrows, place a pencil in a vertical position beside your nose and the inside corner of your eye. This is where the eyebrow should begin. Next place the pencil diagonally from the side of the nose to the outside corner of the eye. This is where the eyebrow should end. The beginning and the ending of the eyebrow should be on a horizontal line.

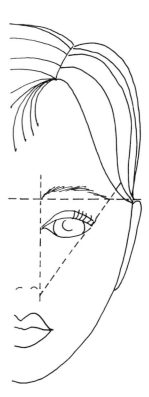

After studying the illustration and your own eyebrows, get an eyebrow brush or a child's toothbrush and a pair of tweezers with diagonal tips. Brush your brows straight up. With the edge of the brush, brush them into their natural shape. The arch should be over the outside edge of the pupil. If you have any stray, "straggly" hairs underneath the natural browline or beyond the points on the illustration, remove them. *Never* remove hairs from *above* the brow. The first time you pluck your brows it may hurt a little and your eyes may water. Be patient. If you remove them correctly, after a couple of times you won't feel any pain. The first time you tweeze your brows, open the pores by steaming your brow area with a washcloth dipped in warm water and wrung out. Pull the stray hair in the direction it grows (this is very important for preventing discomfort). After you have finished, rub the area with a cotton ball saturated with witch hazel. If your brow area looks puffy and red, rub an ice cube quickly over the area.

Once you start tweezing, you must keep it up! So think about it before you begin. Do you really need to tweeze your brows? If you do, start as I have told you. Then to keep it up, check your brows every other morning or so for stragglies. (Do this after you get out of the shower while your pores are still open from the steam.)

The natural color of your brows is usually a little lighter shade of your hair color. That is the way they should be, so don't ever add color to make them darker. If you have thin brows with sparse places in them, you may need to fill in with a pencil or eyebrow powder. Never draw a continuous line for brows. (Yuk! There's that clown look again.) Apply hairlike strokes in the sparse area with a shade a little lighter than your natural brow color. A color the same shade goes on too dark. Soften the pencil or powder you have just applied by very lightly brushing over it with your eyebrow brush. If it still looks too harsh, dust with powder and brush again.

9. EYESHADOWS

Eyes are the big challenge. Since every person's eyes are shaped differently, it's impossible to give ironclad rules for eyeshadow application. This is the area where the artist in you can come out. Experiment. After each new look you give your eyes, look closely in the mirror and then stand at a distance from the mirror. What kind of effect do you get?

Work out one basic make-up look that is the best for your coloring and facial features. If you are choosing the correct clothing colors for yourself, the make-up will work with everything. Once you have a basic look down pat, you may want to experiment with other colors. No, you don't have to match your eyeshadow to your outfit. Just as you don't change your hair color to match your outfit, you don't change your make-up.

Regardless of whether you are a brunette, a blonde, or a redhead, your basic eyeshadows should be muted colors such as grays, taupes, beiges, plums, and other similar colors. The bright shocking colors such as electric blue are best to use in small amounts for accents, such as a dot or "V" subtly blended at the corners of your eyes. If your shadow is too obvious, it is wrong. You want attention to be brought to your eyes, not to your eyelids! There is nothing worse than to see shocking blue or grass green eyelids. You can hardly concentrate on the conversation for looking at those strange, unnatural, brightly colored eyelids.

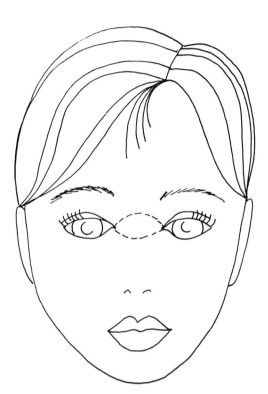

Eyeshadows come in creme, pencil, and pressed-powder forms. I find the easiest to use is the pressed-powder shadow. If you have oily eyelids, apply your oil-free foundation to the eyelid area and powder before you apply your shadow.

Study your eyes. Are they close set, wide apart, or average? Measure the width of one eye. The space between your eyes, across the bridge of your nose, is the same as one eye width if you have average-spaced eyes. If the width between your eyes is wider than one eye, you have wide-set eyes. If it is narrower than one eye, you have close-set eyes.

Close-set eyes. Apply light-colored shadow to the inner part of your eyelid up to the brow. Apply darker shadow to the outer part, blending the two together. Start the liner at the center of the upper and lower eyelids and extend slightly beyond the corner.

Wide-set eyes. Apply dark shadow to the inner part of your eyelid up to the brow. Apply lighter shadow to the outer part, and blend the two together. Line your eye all the way around.

Deep-set eyes. Apply light shadow to the entire area from the lashes to the brow.

Prominent eyelids. Apply dark shadow to the lid and light shadow from the crease to the brow.

Average eyes. Apply a light shadow over the entire lid. Apply a darker shadow over the base shadow on the bone just above the eyelid.

As a rule, the best shadows for you are the colors that are direct complements of your eye color rather than shadows the same color as your eyes. I've noted some colors that are generally good for each season type. You may want to review your color season in the wardrobe section (see page 146).

Color-Keyed Season	Shadow
Spring	Family of yellow browns and peachy browns Family of blue greens
Summer	Family of grays, gray blues, blues, and navy Family of rose and purples
Autumn	Same as Spring plus green/olive family
Winter	Same as Summer plus a cobalt blue

The shadow colors may be from light to dark in each color family. For example, in the family of rose, the shadow color may be a pale pink, a burgundy, or colors in between the two.

If you have some eyeshadow that is too garish, soften it with brown if your skin has warm undertones and with gray if you have cool undertones. Frosted shadows catch the light and draw attention to the area, so be sure not to use them where you are trying to recede an area or camouflage a feature. Anyone can wear a matte eyeshadow, but many people cannot wear the frosted one because of this tendency.

178

10. EYELINER

Eyeliner makes your lashes look thicker, and it defines your eyes. The liner should be smudged so as not to give a harsh line. You can use your darker shade of shadow for a liner, a pencil, a liquid (my least favorite because it has a tendency to go on too thick), or a cake type with water and brush. My favorite is a soft pencil. Use gray or navy for cool undertones and brown or dark green/olive for warm undertones.

Apply close to the lashes with the emphasis on the outer part of the eye, unless your eyes are wide set. Smudge the line with a Q-Tips cotton swab. For special occasions, you can line the ledge of the lower lid with a cobalt blue pencil. It defines the eye with great impact and makes the whites of the eyes look even whiter. Remember, though, you are putting make-up very near your eyes, so be careful and don't do it often.

11. MASCARA

Mascara and blush are the two cosmetics most girls would not want to be without. Your basic mascara is black, brown black, or brown, depending on the intensity of your coloring. If you are fair, you will wear the brown or brown black.

Before applying mascara, you may want to use an eyelash curler. It gives you a wide-open eye look. Be very careful in using the curler. Leave it pressed for just a second. Repeat if necessary.

Powder your eyelashes, and then apply a thin layer of mascara to the underside and topside from root to tips of the upper lashes. Apply to lower lashes. Separate lashes with a brush. (Wash a wand from mascara you have used up and keep for this.) Repeat the process if you want a thicker look. Don't use the eyelash curler again after you have applied mascara. It will damage your lashes.

179

12. LIPS

With your lip pencil, connect the dots

If you use foundation, apply a thin coat over your mouth and then powder before applying your lipstick. This will help your lipstick stay on much longer. It will also prevent "bleeding" (lipstick going into the tiny lines around the mouth). Line your lips with a lip pencil one or two shades darker than your lipstick.

If your lips are too thin, line to the outside edge of your lip line. If they are too full, line to the inside edge of the lip line. Check in the magnifying side of your mirror to be sure your lip liner is balanced and even. Fill in with lipstick.

line narrow lips on outside edge

The lipstick color should be in the same undertone as your coloring—warm or cool. For a special effect, add a touch of gloss to the center of your lower lip.

If you are a preteen or in your early teens, a gloss all over your lips is better than the liner and lipstick. Glosses come in clear as well as tinted shades.

line full lips on inside edge

YOU CAN HAVE A WINNING SMILE

Everyone knows the value of a beautiful smile. In *How To Win Friends and Influence People*, Dale Carnegie lists smiling as his second rule for making people like you. Smiling is your greatest asset. And to help keep your smile bright and your teeth healthy, be sure to brush thoroughly every day—and after every meal and every snack if you wear braces.

Braces are often used to correct malocclusion (problems with the way teeth fit together). Remember, you are wearing braces for a short

180

while now so you can have beautiful, straight, properly fitting teeth for the rest of your life.

Here are some cosmetic tips while wearing braces:

1. Stay away from frosted lipsticks. The shine of the lipstick will emphasize the shine of the braces, and others will notice them more.

2. Don't overemphasize your mouth with a liner or a bold lipstick.

3. Use soft, muted, matte lipsticks.

4. Don't wear shiny jewelry or shiny hair ornaments.

A STEP BY STEP REVIEW

Have fun! Practice and experiment until you learn how to apply your make-up to show off the Best You!

One of the hardest things about make-up is finding the correct colors for your particular coloring and the correct skin care products for your type skin. To take the guesswork out, my company has done that for you. We have available skin care products and color-keyed make-up for teen-age girls. If you are interested in taking advantage of this service please use the order blank on page 192 to receive a brochure describing these products.

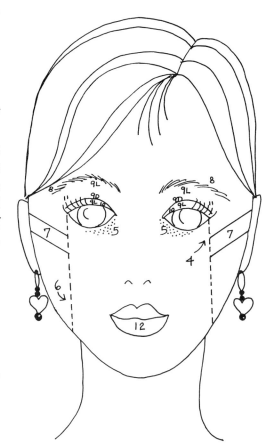

1. cleanse
2. tone
3. moisturize
4. foundation
5. concealer
6. loose face powder
7. blush
8. eyebrows
9. eyeshadow
10. eyeliner
11. mascara
12. lips

181

Tools

- ♥ narrow slant-edged brush
- ♥ eyebrow brush
- ♥ slant-edged tweezers
- ♥ eyelash curler
- ♥ sharpener for eyebrow, eyeliner & lip pencils
- ♥ Q-Tips
- ♥ cotton balls
- ♥ make-up sponge
- ♥ stand-up mirror with magnifying side

Notes
- ♥ make my "face tracing"

CHAPTER SIXTEEN

the best me nail care

♥ Have you ever seen someone whose grooming appeared absolutely flawless, that is, until you saw her hands? The bitten and unkempt fingernails totally ruined the picture she had tried to create. Yes, little things are important too.

Taking good care of your fingernails and toenails is an important part of your beauty routine. Learn how to give yourself a manicure and a pedicure like a professional. You will save both time and money, plus have the advantage of always having great-looking nails! Block out time on your calendar every other week for the following steps.

EIGHT STEPS TO LOVELY FINGERNAILS

Find a well-lighted spot at a table. Put a covering on the table top in case of spills. Lay out all of your tools and materials for the manicure on a towel on the table.

1. REMOVE OLD NAIL POLISH

Moisten a piece of cotton with a good quality nail polish remover. Hold it on the nail for a few seconds, then use a rotary motion and remove the polish. Start with your little finger and work to your thumb.

2. FILE YOUR NAILS

Using an emery board, held at a slight angle to the nail, file one side of the nail and then the other. Do not use a back-and-forth movement. File in one direction only, from the side to the center. File to an oval shape. If you file the sides low and leave a center point, you will weaken the nail.

3. SOAK NAILS IN WARM SOAPY WATER

Using a soft nail brush, clean the nails and cuticle.

4. GENTLY PUSH BACK THE CUTICLE

Dip an orange stick wrapped in cotton or a Q-Tips cotton swab in cuticle remover and push back the cuticle. Scrub nails again with the brush and warm soapy water.

5. BUFF NAILS

If you haven't started wearing nail polish yet, buff your nails to a pretty shine and you have finished your nail manicure! Buff in one direction. (You can buy a nail buffer at a department store or drugstore.)

6. APPLY BASE COAT

Wipe your nails once more lightly with remover to be sure your nails are prepared for the base coat to adhere. Use three strokes, one on each side and one down the center of the nail.

7. APPLY TWO COATS OF POLISH

Use the same procedure with the three strokes for each nail. Remove a hairline of polish from the tip of each nail. (With a tissue stretched across the end of your index finger, rub along the end of the polished nail.) This will help prevent chipping. Wait five minutes between each application of polish.

Your polish should be no darker than your lipstick and in the same undertone. If you are cool, your nail polish will be cool undertone. If you are warm, your nail polish will be warm undertone. You may want to wait until you are older to wear the very bright or deep nail colors. Stay with the pretty pale or transparent colors for now.

8. APPLY A SEALER

Brush a colorless sealer over the nail and under the tip of the nail. Apply a sealer every other day and your manicure will last up to two weeks if you take good care of your hands. (Wear rubber gloves when doing dishes.)

Be sure to give yourself another manicure when needed. Nails with colored polish take more upkeep than nails which have been buffed and left natural or nails with clear polish. Be realistic about the amount of time you want to spend on your nails.

THREE STEPS TO A LUXURIOUS PEDICURE

The procedure for giving yourself a pedicure is basically the same as for a manicure with the following exceptions.

1. Your toenails should be cut or filed straight across, rather than in an oval shape.

2. After soaking your feet, rub them with a pumice stone to smooth rough spots.

3. Using a toe separator (you can buy it at a department store) or cotton rolls, separate your toes before polishing the nails.

FOR BEAUTIFUL, SOFT HANDS AND FEET

Now that your nails have been taken care of, treat your hands and feet to a beauty ritual. Before going to bed, rub them generously with petroleum jelly and put on old white gloves and socks. Go to sleep and wake up the next morning with hands and feet as soft as a baby's skin! You are ready now to put your best hands and feet forward!

Notes

♥ give myself a "professional" manicure + pedicure

Tools

♥ emery boards
♥ toenail clippers
♥ cotton balls
♥ Q-Tips or orangewood sticks
♥ towel
♥ bowl or pan for warm sudsy water

Materials

♥ nail polish remover
♥ base coat polish
♥ nail polish
♥ clear top coat polish

CHAPTER SEVENTEEN

the best me--
the very best me

♥ Becoming the Best Me is a possible dream. By putting into practice the principles presented in this book, the inner and outer Best Me can become a reality. Hard work will be required, but the joy of becoming the very Best Me is truly exhilarating!

YOU HAVE INVALUABLE WORTH

On many occasions I have had the opportunity to witness a transformation in teen-age girls. What a rare joy when a human being like yourself, unique in all of human history, begins to find herself and grow in a healthy, mature way. If this book can help you see your invaluable worth and your ability to matter in life, I will consider it a success.

Now that you've finished reading the material, go back and reread and restudy it. Work on that healthy and realistic image of yourself. Hold on to it, dream about it, build on it, and never let go!

Remember, you can do something about those possible dreams. Please don't waste your precious time and energy struggling with impossible dreams that can never come true. The talents, intellect, emotions, and body that God has given you can all be enhanced and embellished. That requires something of you. Most worthwhile things in this life require a struggle. Be prepared to work at becoming the very best you can be.

BE PATIENT

But don't get overanxious. Learning to type or play a piano requires discipline and practice, and so do the things we have talked about here. Some may come slowly, some rapidly, but all will come through persistence and determination. Just as a master painting required the planning, discipline, and work of the master painter, so does the master Best Me. Remember, the finished work will be well worth the effort.

Envision your inner self as confident, poised, relaxed, bright, and fun to be with. What great satisfaction you will have when you see the real *you* come alive! Everyone will notice! As you discover that you are really an exciting and interesting person, others will find you that way too! You will move to a new level in your life.

And what about that outer you? Can you see your appearance coming alive and blossoming? I know you can! And isn't it something to see that the outer you is really beginning to mirror the inner you? The radiance of the inner self never fails to express itself in the outer self.

As you master this image building of the inner and outer you, you will have gained something that will last long after this book! You will have become all you have the potential to be!

"The Teen I Want to Be" is the Best Me, the very Best Me.

Become

"The Teen

You

Want to Be"

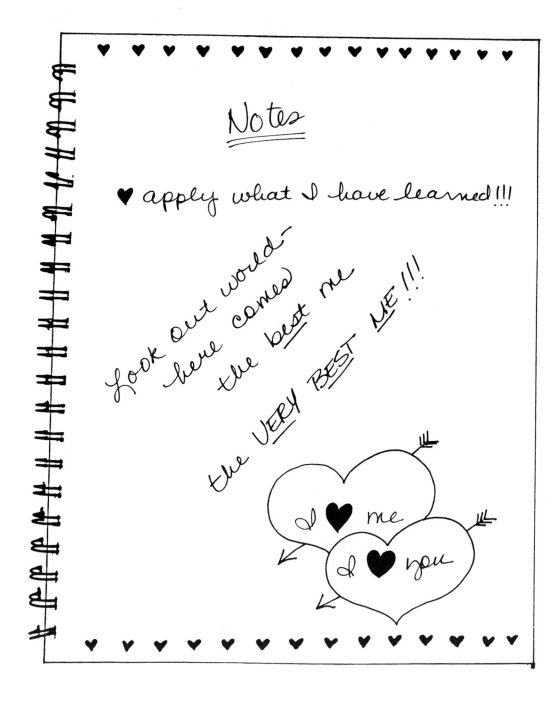